Advance Praise for Laura Resnick's
Rejection, Romance and Royalties

"Over the past few years, I have become a connoisseur of Laura Resnick's column. Her witty comments on the struggles a writer faces in today's world of publishing are refreshingly insightful. A welcome voice in an often solitary profession."

-*JEAN AUEL, bestselling author of* Clan of the Cave Bear

"*Rejection, Romance and Royalties* is the best book on the writing life since *Bird By Bird* or *The Artist's Way.* The incisive and insightful Laura Resnick cuts right to the heart of the joys, sorrows, costs, and rewards of pursuing the creative dream."

-*TERESA MEDEIROS,* New York Times *bestselling author*

"Laura Resnick is as sharp, funny, honest, and insightful a writer about the writing business and the art of being a writer as anyone I know. Personally, I'm putting in my order for this collection of her articles now, because my tattered copies are in serious danger of wearing out."

-*ANNE HOLMBERG, award-winning romance author published under the pennames Anne Avery and Kate Holmes*

"Anyone who's ever done battle with the IRS or tried to outsmart the voodoo of computer technology will identify with Laura Resnick's hilarious hijinks. You'll howl with laughter at her wit, nod with appreciation for her savvy!"

-*SHIRL HENKE, bestselling author of 24 novels*

"The writing life is tough, but Resnick rants with such style and laugh-out-loud humor that readers will enjoy the suffering."

-*PATRICIA RICE, award-winning author of 35 novels*

"For three wonderful years, the first page I turned to when receiving my *Nink* was [Resnick's column]. Laura expressed, as few others can, all that it means to be a novelist, especially of genre fiction. She made me laugh. She made me groan. And she never failed to somehow make me feel better about what I do."

-*ROBIN LEE HATCHER, bestselling author of over 40 novels*

"Laura Resnick's trenchant commentaries on writers and writing capture the passion, perils, and pitfalls of publishing. She invites readers into the mind and heart of the writer, a journey certain to fascinate, instruct, and inspire."

-CAROLYN HART, *author of 34 mysteries*

"Laura Resnick's columns are witty, clever, cogent, and most important—they are important advice on how to survive as a writer. Getting published is only half of it: learning how to live in an erratic industry is the other, and Resnick provides advice on how to do that in spades—and hearts, and laughter."

-EDITH LAYTON, *award winning author of over 25 historical romances and two dozen novellas*

"As an observer of the human condition, Laura Resnick both amuses and delights. More importantly, she has an intimate understanding of the creative process and the agonies and ecstasies of the artistic soul."

-R.J. KAISER, *author of 14 mystery-thriller novels*

"Resnick's wit and wisdom constitute an indispensable survival guide for the professional writer."

-NICOLE BYRD, *award-winning author of historical romance*

"I *depend* on Laura Resnick's rants. They give me comfort and inspiration, laughs and second thoughts."

- GENELL DELLIN, *award-winning author of 25 novels*

"Like Mary Poppins and her 'spoonful of sugar,' Laura Resnick's column makes it a little easier to swallow some of the disappointments the writing business dishes out. She makes me laugh when I want to cry."

-CAROLE BELLACERA, *award-winning novelist*

"Resnick's column is always insightful and incisive. Oh, yes, and irreverent and irresistible for those who are published and those who want (desperately) to be."

-KAREN HARPER, New York Times *bestselling author*

REJECTION
Romance
& ROYALTIE$

The **Wacky World**
of a Working Writer

■■■

LAURA RESNICK

jefferson
press

jefferson press

P.O. Box 115
Lookout Mtn., TN 37350

www.jeffersonpress.com

CONTENTS

This book is dedicated to my dad,

science fiction writer Mike Resnick,

who taught me by example

how to be a filthy pro.

Foreword

A couple of years ago, a savvy, amiable, prolific writer who'd been a national bestseller when I sold my first book called me to talk shop. She had lost her publisher and spent the past couple of years trying to break back into the business; this is not exactly the future one imagines for a hardworking bestseller. More recently, a writer who had returned home from meetings with her publisher in a highly optimistic mood due to their glowing enthusiasm for her work...phoned to tell me she was leaving that house without a new deal; the publisher's "enthusiasm" had translated into a disastrously low offer and poor contract terms, and no amount of negotiation by her agent could get them to budge.

As Hemingway once said, the business of writing makes horse-racing seem like a solid, stable profession.

One day an acquaintance contacted me for help. Out of the blue, a highly respected editor at a major publishing house had approached her and suggested she develop a proposal for a fiction series based on a short story she had published in a little-known market. She did so, and now there was a two-book offer on the table and a promising professional future opening up before her. It was happening so fast and unexpectedly, she hadn't had time to research all the business details she needed to know, so she was (quite sensibly) calling a few people with more experience to walk her through the process.

So it's not as if *only* bad stuff happens in the publishing wilderness.

As I write this, I am awaiting monies for work I did years ago, and I haven't the slightest idea when the checks will arrive, nor how much they will be for; this is the semi-annual ritual of our profession which is known as "collecting royalty payments." I once received a phone call from an editor apologetically informing me that he had never actually sent me the check he'd told me he was sending *two months* earlier, and which I needed to pay my bills (and, of course, the IRS). Due to various mishaps with the postal service, I actually finished writing the entire manuscript of my fourth book several weeks before receiving the contract or my initial advance payment for it (the payment upon which the writer supposedly lives while writing the book).

So you can see how being a writer makes financial planning more than a little challenging on a daily basis.

Conventional wisdom would suggest that a talented, hard-working writer who assiduously pursues an intelligent career goal will probably attain it, and that once you're a bestseller, you've "made it." Common sense would lead one to believe that a book that prints and ships many copies, supported by a massive promotional budget, is bound to be a big success.

As it happens, though, conventional wisdom and common

sense seem to apply less often than Chaos Theory does to the wacky world of the working writer. One talented novelist may follow a well-planned career path all the way to the top of the *New York Times* hardcover list, while another winds up standing on a busy street corner holding a placard that says, "Will Write For Food."

And that's what this book is about: the wacky world of the working writer. I can't show you the Secret Handshake that will lead to overnight bestsellerdom and critical acclaim for your first-ever novel; but I can tell you an awful lot about being a working novelist and surviving for years in this business, both creatively and commercially.

I have sold more than twenty books (though there are one or two that I don't admit to, not even on my website), about sixty short stories, and dozens of columns and articles. I have been a full-time, self-supporting writer for eighteen years. I've worked with four agents, more editors than I can count, and more publishing houses than is good for one's sanity.

As a columnist and essayist, I have been a contributor to *Nink*, the monthly journal of Novelists, Inc., a national organization of professional novelists; to the *SFWA Bulletin*, the national quarterly magazine of the Science Fiction Writers of America; and to the *Romance Writers Report*, the national monthly magazine of the Romance Writers of America. This book is a collection of some of those articles and columns, all of them written by a working writer (affectionately known in some quarters as a "filthy pro") for an audience of writers, both aspiring and professional.

If you're a working writer, I hope you'll find something in these pages to amuse, console, inspire, or refresh you as you continue your daily quest across the River of Fire, through the Plains of Despair, toward the Mountain of Doom in hopes of collecting the Funds of Liberation. (You can tell I'm a fantasy writer, can't you?) If you're an aspiring writer, then I hope this book can teach you what it is to be one of us—and perhaps make you a little better prepared for the shocks of our profession than most of us were when we entered it.

So fasten your seatbelts, and let's begin our bumpy, wild ride into the jungle of professional fiction writing.

The Luck Myth

I recently read a letter to the editor in a publishing trade journal wherein an aspiring writer, amidst various complaints about her hard lot, expressed hope that she would someday be among those of us "lucky enough to have sold a book."

I see this sort of thing often. (And not just from aspirants, alas.) Someone's "lucky" to be a pro, to sell novels, to break into hardcover, to crack the bestseller lists, to get a six-figure advance, to have two publishers, to be under contract for four books, to work steadily for years, and so on.

Newsflash: Luck is the least of the things you need to survive and succeed as a professional writer. Few things are more self-defeating in the aspiring writer, more pointless in the embittered pro, and more insulting to the steadily working novelist than perpetuating "the Luck Myth."

The Luck Myth is the rationalization whereby a dissatisfied writer blames bad luck and an unfair world for his not having what he wants, whether it's a first professional sale or a string of hardcover bestsellers; as a corollary, the Luck Myth also involves attributing someone else's success, whether it's a modest short story sale or a six-figure advance for a novel, to luck (and an unfair world, of course).

Now don't get me wrong: I think luck is wonderful! Send me a bushel, I won't turn it down. But luck is very elusive—far too elusive to form the foundation of a career plan—and therefore mostly irrelevant in the overall scheme of a filthy pro's life. As award-winning science fiction novelist Catherine Asaro says, "I wouldn't say luck played any part in my writing career. Persistence and hard work were the determining factors. I never gave up, no matter how many times I was told, 'You can't do that.'"

New York Times bestselling romance novelist Mary Jo Putney once remarked to me that "luck" is really a matter of a writer working hard and creating chances for opportunities to come her way. Or, as Victoria Thompson reminds me, "Luck is when opportunity meets preparation." Thompson was cast off by a down-sizing publisher several years ago, an event that forced her to get a day job after years of writing romance full-time. It was dogged persistence, not luck, she explains, that helped her resurrect her writing career and, after a couple of years, become an Edgar-nominated mystery novelist. Kristine Kathryn Rusch, a mystery, romance, and science fiction/fantasy writer, considers persistence the most important factor in maintaining a long-term career: "No matter how much shit they throw at you, and they will...you must pick yourself up, dust yourself off, and try again." As Jennifer Roberson, author of numerous historical and fantasy novels, says, "Without persistence, ninety-nine percent of us wouldn't have careers."

Which is not to negate the importance of talent, of course. Mary Jo Putney and I occasionally ponder together, "What's more important: talent or persistence?" We invariably come to the conclusion that talent is more important—but useless, in the majority of cases, *without* persistence. As Jennifer Roberson, who spent fifteen years trying to break into the business, notes, "Without persistence, the most brilliantly talented writer in the world may never be published." Meanwhile, Putney and I have often agreed that real persistence combined with only very modest talent can keep you working for years. Luck, we both admit, is really nice, and a little luck occurs in most careers (including both of ours); but luck runs far behind talent and persistence as a very distant third-place finish.

Toni Blake, author of more than half a dozen romance novels, concurs, noting that luck comes in "way behind both talent and persistence. As a person who wrote twelve romances before selling one, and twenty before selling to the market I was targeting, I think I'm proof of that." Or, as bestselling science fiction/fantasy writer Kevin J. Anderson quotes to me, "The harder I work, the luckier I get."

Ernest Hemingway once said, "Anyone who says he wants to be a writer and isn't writing, doesn't." So when I decided I wanted to become a writer, the first thing I did was write three novels. I didn't get online and spend my writing time grumbling about how hard it was to be an aspiring writer. (Okay, I couldn't; I'd never even *heard* of the Internet back then. Yes, it was a long time ago.) I didn't join a writers group and sit around talking about writing. I didn't bore my friends by telling them how I was planning to write. As E.L. Doctorow said, planning, researching, and talking about writing aren't writing; only *writing* is writing. So I wrote.

(However, I'm forced to admit that three books is pretty bush-league. My friend Lori Foster, bestselling author of more than thirty published novels, completed ten books as an aspiring writer.)

After completing my second book, I started querying literary agents. Eleven agents in a row rejected me. Roughly half of them told me I had no talent and couldn't write. The other half told me the romance genre was dead, and I hadn't a hope in hell of selling to it.

Gosh, is that *unlucky*, or what?

Well, no. *New York Times* bestseller Kevin J. Anderson— author of more than seventy published novels, with more than fifteen million copies of his books in print—collected eighty rejection slips before making his first sale. As Anderson notes, most aspiring writers give up well before they acquire eighty rejection slips, "But I had persistence (at the time, I think my parents called it 'foolish stubbornness')." His collection now has a total of about 800 rejection slips in it, so it exceeds mine; however, I don't write as fast as Kevin, so I can't get rejected as often—simple cause and effect. "One of the awards I have prominently displayed in my office," Anderson says, "is a trophy with the engraved plaque, 'The Writer With No Future,' which I received because I could produce the most rejection slips, by weight, of any writer at an entire conference." Sitting next to this award, by the way, is his Guiness World Record certificate, received some years later, for setting the record for the World's Largest Single-Author Book Signing. Which is an inspiring example of what can happen if you're foolishly stubborn as well as very talented.

As bestseller John Jakes once said, "Too many beginning writers give up too easily." Or, to quote Richard Bach, author of *Jonathan Livingston Seagull*, "A professional writer is an amateur who didn't quit."

Giving up didn't occur to me, and so I broke into the business. I remained with my first publisher for a number of years, during which time I sold them a total of eleven books. However, I submitted many more than that. They rejected any number of my proposals—once, as many as four in a row. However, I just kept patching my wounds, writing new work, and submitting something else. It certainly helped that I had learned a valuable lesson very early in my career which I never forgot:

One thing that really puzzled me when I broke into the business was that a surprising number of writers who'd sold books before I ever came along seemed to have disappeared from publishing. Poof! Just gone, with no reasonable explanation (such as death, for example). This really spooked me. Did that mean that one day—poof!—*I* would be "just gone," too?

Then, by chance, I met one of these "just gone" writers. We were introduced by a mutual acquaintance and had lunch together. I wondered how to broach the subject of her complete disappearance from the business after three books. Fortunately, I didn't need to bring it up; she was, in fact, eager to talk about it and expectant of earning my commiseration. She and her editor had had some disagreements about revisions on the third book; then the editor rejected her fourth book. *Voilà!* End of this author's career. She was wounded and furious, and she never submitted another book there or anywhere else. Ever again.

After I processed that information, I became incredibly relieved and lost all fear of disappearing from the business. Lo and behold, there was nothing mysterious about the writers who disappeared forever after one book, three books, a handful of short stories, whatever. All they did was...*give up*. Quit! Stopped trying with all their might. Some of them may have quit as easily as this woman, who disappeared from the business on the basis of one sole rejection. Others may have quit after being dumped by a publisher (which is different than a rejection; when you're dumped, the publisher terminates the relationship and advises you not to submit to them again). Or they may have quit after having a publisher fold underneath them, or after having four books in a row rejected, or after being dumped by an agent.

You know why I've worked steadily for more than fifteen years in this business? I'd like to attribute it to my charm (but you'd know I was lying), and I'll take credit for at least some talent; but the only reason I'm still standing is that I didn't give up, quit, or stop trying. Not when I was dumped by a publisher. Not when three (not one, not two, but *three*) publishers folded underneath me. Not when my first agent dumped me. Not when I wrote two, three, or four proposals in a row that got rejected. I didn't give up when my second editor (who inherited me from my first, who quit the business) went months without reading my work or answering my calls, and made it clear she considered me nothing but extra work which she had no intention of doing. I didn't stop trying when I wrote book proposals that were turned down by every editor in the free world. I didn't quit when half a dozen publishers rejected my first "big" romance novel; which is good, because it eventually sold for my biggest-ever advance up until then. I didn't give up in despair when my third agent suggested twice in a row that I revise my first fantasy proposal before he tried to sell it. (Which is also a good thing, because that proposal led to a multi-book hardcover deal and my biggest-ever advance at that time.) In fact, I actually tried to quit writing twice and found that I just couldn't.

I'm still here because I persist. Talent certainly helps me sell my work, and I've occasionally had a stroke of luck. But if I didn't constantly write and submit, look for new opportunities, write and submit, create new opportunities, write and submit, prepare and plan, then I'd probably never have broken into the business, and I certainly wouldn't have survived in it, let alone achieved any level of success.

Scratch the surface of steadily working professional writers, and you'll find many who wrote numerous stories and books before selling one, who spent years trying to break in, who collected piles of rejection slips before making that first sale. Get any successful writer into deep discussion about her career (and her friends' careers), and you'll hear tales of six-figure contracts cancelled because books were deemed "unpublishable," high-profile releases that descended into plummeting sales figures and two years without work, promising publishing relationships which petered out into bad marketing plans and unreturned phone calls, rejection letters of withering distaste, revision letters of soul-crushing negativity, publishers folding, imprints crashing, etc., etc.

This is the business; and you stay active in it by persisting, not by being lucky.

Meanwhile, if all you do is talk about writing without actually writing and submitting a whole lot, or if your first couple of books are rejected everywhere you send them and you stop writing and submitting, or if no professional market will buy your first six short stories and you stop writing so you can spend more time grumbling, or if your editor rejects your next book and you just sit around and mope about it for ten years, or if your publisher asks you never to darken their door again and you sob into your cashmere sweater about this for five years…guess what will happen?

That's right: *Nothing.*

I, meanwhile, will still be getting "lucky."

The Reader's Mighty Pen

I sit by myself in my office day after day, all alone with a book that requires months upon months of effort, drive, commitment, and vision (as well as large quantities of chocolate and coffee). I write, I rewrite, I revise, I hone, I wash, I dry, I ventilate. No one is present for my moments of weary despair, my flashes of insight, or my sudden forehead-slapping solutions to problems that have plagued the work for weeks.

When the book is finally done, polished, and tweaked to the very best of my ability, I deliver it to my editor and (drum roll, please)...I get a revision letter. Not awards, not ovations, not the roar of the crowd. No, I get told about all the ways in which the work is inadequate and in need of improvement.

Talk about an anti-climactic response to a heroically sustained effort.

By the time a book goes out into the marketplace, I've already been numbed by the events which have greeted it ever since delivery: editing, payment delays, copy editing, production, packaging, cover copy, more delays, shipping, etc.

Then come the reviews. No matter how many people praise the book, you can always count on at least one reviewer (or perhaps a lot of them) feeling honor-bound to trash it thoroughly in print for all the world to see—or perhaps just pointedly ignore it as beneath his notice.

So one day you're thinking, "Why do I bother? What was I thinking? Why didn't I become a lawyer, or a stripper, or a lion tamer instead of a writer? I could've had class, I could've been a contender!" And just as you're rethinking your professional choices and ordering a sequin-covered G-string...you get a letter like this:

"I am nineteen years old and really never liked reading. But for some reason I bought your book and I was totally engulfed in it. I would find myself reading for hours on end. And that's real rare in me. It takes a special kind of book to do that. I think I have only enjoyed two maybe three books in my life, but yours blew them all away...You made [me an] avid reader and [now I] am eagerly awaiting your next book."

And suddenly, even lion taming doesn't seem as appealing as sitting down to write your next book, your next chapter, your next page, your next word. Because you've been reminded that people are *reading* what you write, people care, people want more—and a big part of what made you a writer, a filthy pro, is the drive to tell your tales to others.

Learning that I turned a non-reader into an avid reader was one of the most rewarding moments of my career. At a moment like that, I think, *wow*, despite the many rejection letters, the occasional snide review, the publishers lost, the public disappointments, the private fears, the dismissive comments, and the missing checks, I'm doing something worthwhile here. I have every reason to persist and persevere. Someone out

there who doesn't even know me has written to urge me to
keep writing, because my work speaks to him. Could anything
be better?

Some of my readers are apologetic about writing to me,
saying they're sure I get pestered by far too much fan mail
(yeah, right) and don't need yet another reader bothering
me, but they were so engaged by something I wrote that they
nonetheless felt they had to contact me. Several have even
apologized for being so "disrespectful" as to ask when the
next book is coming out, because they just can't wait. Some
have written to ask me, always very politely, to further build
on certain characters or certain aspects of previous work.
And even those readers who don't feel they must apologize
for "disturbing" me with their approbation nonetheless have
no idea just how much their comments mean to me. More
than I can ever say—even though I get paid to know how to
say things.

However, despite how moving or rewarding most of our
reader mail is, we've all also received...The Other Kind of mail.

Though I would never say so in my responses to them,
a few well-meaning readers have unwittingly made me
wince when intending to compliment me. It typically goes
something like this: "You and [insert the name here of the
author whose writing you most dislike] are my two favorite
writers in the whole world." Or: "Your recent novel is right
up there alongside [insert the name of the most offensive or
badly-written novel you've read in the past ten years] as the
best I've ever read."

Sometimes, I confess, this effusive praise makes me
contemplate sticking my head in a lion's mouth as a worthy
professional use of my brain. But I know I should accept such

a compliment in the generous spirit with which it is given. (Conversely, novelist Lillian Stewart Carl once received a letter in which the reader asked if she also wrote under another name...which just happened to be the name of one of my favorite novelists. Now *that's* a flattering comparison!)

However, some readers don't mean well, and their letters are intentionally insulting. For example, fantasy novelist Kate Elliot received this charming missive from a reader: "i just finished reading volume three of your crown of stars. please return alains dignity back to him, he is the sole reason im reading your too long and very boring story." Happily, Elliot kept her sense of humor upon reading this. Considering that her books are each several hundred thousand words long, that is, as she notes, "a lot of pages to read, considering how 'boring' it is!"

A reader wrote to inform a friend of mine, "I sure *don't* want any more of your books if they are as '*Boring*' as this one was." Another writer I know received a letter from a reader telling him that he'd only ever written one novel good enough for the reader *not* to trade it in at the local used bookstore.

Are we having fun yet?

Some readers are distressed by a novel and want to let the writer know. Bestselling novelist Nora Roberts once got a letter castigating her for killing a cat in *Montana Sky*. "No mention was made," Roberts says, "of the human beings who'd been scalped, sliced, and disemboweled [in the book]. But I'd killed a cat. I was a terrible person, and she was never, never reading me again." Novelist Tamar Myers received a four-page letter from a Canadian member of the Monarchist Society castigating her for making a joke (in one of her books) about Her Majesty's clothes. He sent a copy of the letter to Buckingham Palace where, he assured Myers, the likes of her will never be invited for tea. Award-winning romance novelist Jo Beverley sometimes hears from readers who think it's *her* fault that some of her novels are out of print and hard to find. One reader, in particular, wrote a comment along the lines of, "Curse you, Jo Beverley, and curse your publishers for your cruelty!"

And sometimes readers just want to share a little too much. My friend Lisa Ann Verge received a letter wherein a reader had experienced the same medical emergency which had occurred in one of Verge's books. "Her husband hadn't reacted quickly enough, however," Verge says, "and now she doesn't trust him. Divorce papers are in the mail." Another reader wrote to novelist Kristine Kathryn Rusch: "I was planning to fly to Oregon to take you out for a nice dinner. I think we might be compatible." However, the reader said, he'd changed his mind about wooing Rusch, based on the (erroneous) assumption that she was the "girl" of co-author Kevin J. Anderson. In an unrelated incident, Anderson received a letter from a young fan demanding the author send him several thousand dollars, explaining at length why he needed the money more than Anderson did.

Writer Lynn Flewelling hears from homophobic fundamentalists from time to time—who are usually astonished to discover that she's a church-goer (a background which they apparently don't associate with tolerance and compassion). And on one memorable occasion, Flewelling received a lengthy letter telling her she was threatening the fabric of American society with her books. It might have upset her more, of course, had the letter's author not been a prison inmate.

Speaking of which, what *is* it about prison inmates? Do they just have a lot of time on their hands? Or is prison where fanatic readers are all destined to wind up? Romance writer Cassandra Austin seems to have a genuine following in prisons, as did a bestseller I know who moved her post office box to another city after receiving dozens of letters from men serving time. My friend Lisa Verge's most ardent fan is a Nigerian prisoner in Thailand. He's a lifer in Bangkok due to trying to support his many sisters in a way the Thai government didn't like, and he's written to Verge several times about her various books.

Prison inmates notwithstanding, sometimes Close Encounters of the Deeply Weird Kind begin innocently. Nora Roberts received several letters from a young woman in Nigeria who asked for some books because she had no money and very little access to booksellers. Roberts sent her a couple of books. In retrospect, this was perhaps a mistake. Shortly thereafter, Roberts says, "I got a letter from her requesting I buy her a pair of red silk pants, size medium. Good quality, if I didn't mind, and she'd like them before Christmas. If this was inconvenient, I could just send her a hundred US dollars, and she'd take care of the shopping. While I was at it, could I find her a nice Moslem boy?" Apart from the difficulties inherent in finding a nice Moslem boy in rural Maryland, Roberts says she stops short of sending money and men to her readers. (Go figure.) So their correspondence ended there.

Some of the most peculiar mail comes—predictably, perhaps—as a result of writing about UFOs. After publishing a short story about UFOs, Russell Davis received a letter explaining to him that UFOs aren't alien spaceships at all. No, indeed. They're angels and demons battling in the sky for possession of human souls, and the writer would do well to learn that fact before writing about them again. Anne Marie Winston, after writing a book wherein two characters are abducted by aliens, received a seven-page letter from a reader who wasn't from "here" (planet Earth). Winston says, "She pointed out all the fallacies in my book (like the fact that aliens don't lower a ramp to get us on board—how stupid of me) and explained in great detail how the world would end on December 31st of that year…Those among us—like her—who were really 'planted here' would be taken back while the rest of us poor dopes perished." (Here's hoping my next publishing check gets here before the big day.)

However, despite the occasionally strange or nasty ones, most reader letters are a delightful boon to the weary writer whose usual reward for writing a book is…a revision letter. (Or deafening silence. Or a rejection. Or a refusal to accept and publish the manuscript. Or a demand from the IRS for a piece of the action. But I digress.)

And some of these letters are incredibly rewarding, making up for a lot of the crap that professional writers daily endure. Novelist Susan Wiggs received these comments from a teenager who'd read one of her books: "You changed my life, and my whole perspective on the world. I would not be the person I am today without you. You have a tremendous gift…You can make a person's life better, simply by writing with your born skill for writing. I'm living proof of that. Thank you."

"Do you take good care of yourself?" one reader's lovely letter asks me. "Do you look both ways before you cross the street and drink lots of water and get regular check-ups? I sure would be disappointed if something happened to you before you finished writing down everything that you have to say."

Reader mail can keep us going when the tunnel, far from having a light at the end of it, is actually caving in on us and releasing toxic gas fumes while trapping us beneath rubble. Letters from our readers remind us that, for good or for ill, we are not nearly as alone with our work as we usually feel we are. And for every reader who makes an unreasonable demand or who insults us, there are also those whose letters remind us why we write—so they will read us.

Passion

"Technique alone is never enough.
You have to have passion."
—Raymond Chandler

The other day, I was watching the Chandleresque, hard-boiled thriller, *L.A. Confidential*. Guy Pearce plays an intelligent young cop who discovers that he has become corrupted by ambition. In a confessional conversation about this, Pearce talks about what made him become a cop: He wanted to catch the bad guys who thought they could get away with it. Then he asks Kevin Spacey, who plays a shrewd, morally corrupted cop, why *he* became one. A sad, surprised look washes across Spacey's face as he says, "I don't remember."

I am a shrewd, emotionally corrupted writer, and, some days, I don't remember, either. I have forgotten many times why I became a novelist. It's often a challenge to keep remembering why I write.

It is the heavy reality of the writing life which makes the

"why" so easy to forget: Gutless rejection letters, denigrating revision letters, incompetent copy edits, insulting reviews, late checks, disappointing sales, down-trending print-runs, shrinking advances, royalties paid in a geological timeframe, imprints folding, publishers downsizing their lists and conglomerating their overhead.

One day your editor expresses all the enthusiasm of an overtired undertaker. The next day your agent demonstrates all the faith and commitment of a diseased streetwalker. Your book is packaged with a cover that would embarrass anyone who wasn't raised in a Red Light district. You give a thoughtful interview only to discover the resultant article describes you as churning out potboilers. Three people show up at your book signing, two of them because they thought you were someone else; the third person came because you owe him money. When you make the *New York Times* list, a neighbor asks you "which" *NYT* list you're on, because there must be a separate one for the trash *you* write. Though you've been publishing regularly for years, you know people who ask, every single time they see you, if you still write. (No, I fell back on my independent wealth when the going got tough.)

More than one writer has discovered that a handshake deal with a publisher turned out to be worth less than the paper it never got printed on; and, hey, raise your hand if even the stuff that got written down didn't get honored—gosh, imagine that! Publishers which require sacked employees to vacate the premises immediately, accompanied by a security escort, nonetheless object to writers who request that their earnings not be turned over to agents whom they have fired. Writers have delivered work to editors only to be told it was "unpublishable," "unacceptable," or "unsalvageable." Even in cases where the editors have clearly been wrong (ex. the book sells elsewhere for a good advance and goes on to get award nominations), they nonetheless do it again to someone else. Because, what, if they keep refusing to publish books, they'll eventually get it right?

Editors have told me that my advance is more than I'm worth; my work isn't that good; I should write more like so-and-so; my work is "shit;" I don't know how to write; my work is an "insult" to them; and I don't "appreciate" them enough. Agents have told me I'm "not worth" their time; my query is an insult to them; I'm "self-destructive" (based on my choosing to fire that agent); they "hate" my work; and I'm "lazy" (I wrote a mere 1,400 pages that year).

And people wonder why I've become a little harsh on the subject of publishers, editors, and agents over the years.

You sweat blood, tears, and guts over a manuscript for six months or two years, only to have it rejected everywhere it's submitted, or to see your own publisher treat it so carelessly that people start saying to you, "There *must* be a personal vendetta against you there. Things have gone past the point where so many screw-ups on a book could be sheer coincidence."

And just when you're teetering on the brink of insanity, hovering at the edge of reason, clinging to the last shreds of your self-respect...someone tells you how *lucky* you are to be a professional novelist.

(Bartender! Over here, please!)

You *bet* I sometimes can't remember why I came to this party.

"My muse is a stubborn bitch.
She's showing up on her terms, not on mine."
—Anne Stuart

As paid professionals with contractual obligations, commercial pressures, and financial needs, many of us know the feeling of the well running dry, the enthusiasm being smothered, the spirit getting withered. Maybe we've experienced it ourselves at various points in our career *(I* have, anyhow); or maybe you've only seen friends go through it, even if you've (so far) escaped it yourself.

Yet I remember writing my first three manuscripts in a fever, over a period of less than one year. I was so absorbed in the stories, I would sometimes cancel fun social things for the pleasure of staying home and writing more. I always looked forward to sitting down with my writing. I often completely lost track of time or reality, writing for hours after I should have gone to bed, or for twenty minutes past when I should have left for work.

I have never recaptured the innocent rush of delight I experienced while working on my first few manuscripts as an unpublished, unknown amateur. (As wise novelist Robyn Carr once said to me, "You can't be a virgin twice.") It was like falling in love. It was the pleasure and the fun of the work that kept me going in the absence of any obligation, encouragement, contract, money, kudos, or other external reasons to keep going. It was the *passion.*

Now, please note, I was writing with every intention of seeking publication. I specifically chose to write short series-romance because, at that time (the late 1980s), that subgenre seemed to offer the best possibility of selling something I thought I might actually be able to write: a very short novel about two likeable people falling in love. So even then, my writing involved ambition and commercial-world baggage. I did not start writing for self-expression (you can't seriously imagine that *I* have ever struggled to express myself in the normal course of events). I didn't even start writing for personal satisfaction. I started writing because I wanted to sell a book. So I can't ever say that the desire to be published is necessarily the wrong reason or a bad reason to write.

However, that stark ambition did not interfere with my falling in love with writing and becoming compulsive about the stories I was telling. Indeed, had I not experienced all that pleasure, obsession, and satisfaction—all that passion—I doubt I'd ever have finished my first manuscript. I've never been the most disciplined person, and a book is *very* hard work, after all.

Eventually, after too many hours in this chair combined with too many demoralizing experiences in this business, I tried to quit. (Twice, in fact.) But I couldn't do it. The problem wasn't that I couldn't quit the business; it was always that I couldn't quit writing.

And the thing is, if I'm going to write—and I am, I can't give up that passion—then I want to be published. My passion isn't just for writing; I'm also passionate about my work being *read*. It's like cooking a five-course meal that you damn well want appreciative food-lovers to come over and *eat*; otherwise all your hard work, skill, and commitment just go to waste.

So I endure all the garbage that our business inflicts on me. Not just for the passion of writing, but also for the passion of being read. This is what I remind myself when I start wondering (sometimes every damn day) why I became a writer and why I don't just quit when I'm frustrated, unhappy, and demoralized. Passion is the source, the well, the font. It is ground zero. Without my passion, it would indeed be time to pack up and blow this popsicle stand.

But while I have the passion, it's still worth enduring

all the shit that the writing life brings down upon me...even though the rational part of me wants you to hit me repeatedly until I come to my senses and blow this pop stand, anyhow.

> *"The storyteller's own experience of men and things, whether for good or ill...*
> *has moved him to an emotion so passionate that he can no longer keep it shut up in his heart."*
> **—Murasaki Shikibu (c.978-c.1031)**

Not long ago, another writer told me that a romance editor at one of the big houses remarked that she was getting a lot of submissions that were polished and hit their genre marks...but which had no spark and weren't grabbing her at all—submissions that were competent but lackluster, professional but passionless.

I was at a romance writers' conference two years ago, and one of things I noticed is that the vast majority of questions posed by aspiring writers were all about the "rules:" Can I use this or that setting? Can I use this or that profession? This or that time period? Can I write a paranormal element? Could I have a cop and a teen instead of a cowboy and a baby? What length should the book be? How do you feel about subplots? (Well, to be frank, I wouldn't want my sister to marry one.)

It's as if a novel is a punch-card, with some aspiring writers convinced that if they get all twenty holes punched, then they'll win the Secret Handshake. And like a friend of mine who is an award-winning novelist, I find myself thinking, "Where's the passion?" Where's the individuality, the story that only *this* writer can tell, the story that this writer is *obsessed* with telling? Where is the fun? Where is the risk? Where is the storyteller's compulsion?

Not that this phenomenon is restricted to aspiring writers; it exists among frustrated professionals, too. I've seen professional writers asking the same questions in essence, but with the details altered to reflect their own aspirations: What makes a book a lead title? What makes it a bestseller? A blockbuster? If I changed the kidnapping to a mass abduction, would that make the book a Big Commercial Novel?

I have occasionally felt a mad impulse to provide editors with a placard they could simply hold up instead of repeating over and over in their Q&A sessions that there isn't a perfect formula, there isn't a generic answer about what kind of book will enable an aspiring writer to break into the business, propel a midlist writer into a lead slot, or bust a genre leader out into mega-star status.

> *"Part of being a real writer is defending your vision*
> *and not caving in to outside pressures."*
> *—Jennifer Crusie*

In truth, I tend to believe that publishers bring repetitious story questions and passionless submissions upon themselves by actively exhorting a cookie-cutter mentality. While sitting in a workshop audience a few years ago, for example, I was stunned to hear an editor tell us, when asked about Kathleen Eagle's brilliant novel, *Sunrise Song*, that such original work was all very well for a great writer like Eagle, but don't you folks try this at home; *you* should definitely stick to the specific settings, tones, and storylines I'm telling you I want to see.

Gosh, connect the dots and see if *you* can figure out the mystery of passionless manuscripts.

Another editor once told me that although she usually said she was looking for something new and fresh, what she was actually looking for was more of what's selling well this year or what perpetually sells well.

Even if writing-by-numbers sells books in theory, though, I've learned in reality that the result of repressing my passion in favor of publication is invariably that I get *neither* thing: I don't get the passion of writing something I love and believe in; and I can't sell anything but work I love and believe in, anyhow—at least, not for long. So the cookie-cutter mentality is a dead-end for me. Sacrificing my voice, my vision, and my story is a bad choice for me, because it inevitably results in a lose-lose-lose situation: I don't get the sale, the career growth, or the professional break that I want; I end up with weak work which lacks voice, sparkle, depth, individuality, or integrity; and I don't experience the pleasure, the obsession, and the satisfaction—the passion that makes all the crap of the writing life worth enduring.

I'll probably always write with a determined eye on selling and publication, and I'll probably always strive for bigger advances, better packaging, and more readers (whether I'll *get* them remains to be seen). But I have learned, over the course of taking many knockout blows in this ring, that the starting place every single day has to be passion. I can't write well without it, I can't write for long without it, and I believe that I can only achieve success by honoring my vision, my voice, and my stories rather than by attempting to fill out a publisher's checklist, whether it's a real one or one which I merely imagine exists.

As with the evolutionary behavior of a predator filling its special ecological niche on the savannah, the writing process must provide its own reward (the thrill of the chase, the pleasure of the kill, the satisfaction of the feast) in order for the writer to thrive in the hostile environment of the publishing world.

> *"What another would have done*
> *as well as you, do not do it.*
> *What another would have said as well as you,*
> *do not say it; written as well, do not write it.*
> *Be faithful to that which exists nowhere*
> *but in yourself—*
> *and thus make yourself indispensable."*
> —*André Gide*

Copy Edits We Have Known and Hated

If I were a malicious individual, I would take real pleasure today in...

Oh, who am I kidding? I *am* a malicious individual! So I *do* take real pleasure in throwing a few darts at those rarely seen, seldom heard, shadowy figures of the fiction world: COPY EDITORS (I leave it to you to imagine the sinister music).

According to The Slot (www.theslot.com), a website for copy editors that Bill Walsh (author of *Lapsing Into a Comma*) established in 1995, a copy editor's job is to correct errors in grammar, spelling, usage, consistency, and house style. Obviously, this is an important function, a necessary part of the editing process. And I will be fair (just this once) and admit that throughout my career, most of my copy edits have been good—or at least inoffensive enough that I don't really remember them.

Indeed, the unmemorable copy edit is the ideal experience. A good copy editor uses a light touch, rather than heavily stamping the prose with her own voice (or with her fascist,

storm-trooper bootprint, as the case may be). A good copy
editor discovers and alerts you to the occasional small mistake,
inconsistency, or even embarrassment that has been missed
in all the previous edits and revisions of a manuscript. Since
a good copy editor is so valuable (and, alas, so rare), it's not
unknown for authors to request the same copy editor for all
their books once they find a good one. In fact, I once read
that one of my favorite writers used to insist her favorite copy
editor be written into her contracts, as a guarantee, regardless
of which house was publishing her books at the time.

However, a good copy editor—or even an inoffensive
one—is like the relatives who send you a Christmas or Hanuk-
kah card once a year and otherwise leave you alone; you forget
all about how inoffensive they are when you're mired deep in
primal rage over the relatives who never bring back the car they
borrowed without asking—unless they suddenly return without
warning one day because they've decided to move into your
basement.

Perhaps the most volatile reaction to a copy edit that I
ever saw was that of my father, science fiction writer Mike
Resnick. He wrote a novel in which the narrative describes
one character, a leprechaun, as having an Irish accent. The
copy editor went through the entire manuscript and changed
every single word the character spoke which ended in *ing* to
in'. Showin' a surprisin' streak of practicality, Pop went out
and had a "stet" stamp made at the local print shop, rather
than writin' *stet* ("let it stand") a thousand times. And when he
sent the heavily stetted manuscript back to the publisher, he
phoned the executive editor and warned him that if he didn't
make these (stet) changes, Pop would personally fly to New
York and rip his heart out of his chest.

This would be a good example of why I am considered the *nice* Resnick. *I* usually just threaten to hurt editors badly. It's a rare editor who incites me to threats of actual homicide. But I digress.

A manuscript written by novelist Lisa Ann Verge fell into the hands of a similarly compulsive copy editor who added ellipses to the end of *"every single damn sentence* of dialogue," Lisa says...for three hundred fifty pages...(Lisa should have borrowed Pop's stet stamp...) Indeed, there seem to be so many copy editors with a punctuation compulsion that someone should really consider starting a Twelve-Step program for them. Bestseller Jo Beverley's worst copy editing experience was with "the obsessive semi-colon person," a copy editor who added semi-colons to prose the way Bill Gates adds dollars to his net worth. Jo stetted thirty pages before giving up in exhaustion and phoned her editor about the problem. And fair warning: Beware; it seems that this copy editor may still be migrating around the industry; you could be next.

I myself was once victimized by a compulsive comma lover in my seventh book, *Celestial Bodies* (written as Laura Leone). On virtually every page of the manuscript, phrases like "he sat in his favorite thinking chair" were changed to "he sat in his favorite, thinking chair." (I should, have borrowed, Pop's stet, stamp.)

Although the copy editor is expected to make little changes, some copy editors are evidently unaware that the little changes are meant to be (hullo!) *corrections*. In Alice Duncan's historical romance, *Heaven's Promise* (written as Rachel Wilson), the copy editor changed "footpad" to "footpath." Alice says, "I don't know anyone who's ever been attacked by a footpath, but I don't read much horror."

It's those *little* changes that can really get you if you don't carefully read every single damn word of your copy edit—par-

ticularly when you've been assigned a copy editor whose first
language doesn't seem to be English. In another book of mine,
the copy editor changed a description of horses as "animals
born to a herd mentality," which I thought was a pretty standard phrase, to "animals born to a herd mentally." In *Celestial
Bodies* (again), the copy editor changed "There was a sign in the
window: Help Wanted" to "There was a sign in the window:
help wanted." (I'm not making this up.) Failure to correct copy
editor changes like these can convince your friends and family
that your good education was completely wasted on you.

The bigger changes, however, are the truly infuriating
ones. I don't know if some copy editors are frustrated aspiring
writers or just cruel tormentors who enjoy elevating other
people's blood pressure. And more than a few copy editors
seem to be remarkably incompetent amateur historians.

In one of my favorite examples, the copy editor changed
the names of the songs in Alice Duncan's Civil War romance,
Wild Dream. Thus, the musician hero found himself playing
"The Battle Hymn of the Republic" instead of "The Battle
Cry of Freedom"—suddenly changing sides in the war without
warning. In a novel about the theft of JFK's limousine, Randy
Russell wrote a description of JFK's driver's license, the information taken straight from a copy of Kennedy's actual license
as it appeared in a biography; the copy editor changed JFK's
hair color. In a historical romance novella set in Naples, Mary
Jo Putney was obliged to produce a printed folk recipe from her
research when the copy editor protested, "That dish doesn't
have raisins!" When a copy editor insisted on writing a herd of
buffalo into a character's thoughts, Jo Beverley had to explain

that a herd of buffalo wouldn't be the first (or fifth) image to occur to an English Regency heroine.

Nor are such problems the exclusive burden of historical novelists. Carol Cail set a contemporary novel in the Utah desert and soon found her rustic barbed wire fence changed by the copy editor to chain link. In a Dixie Browning book, the copy editor had never heard of "drum fishermen" and changed it to "drunken fishermen." In another novel, Dixie used the old phrase "kicking over the traces," and the copy editor asked, "Traces of what?" Contemporary romance writer Susan Mallery had a copy editor who was mystified by the real-life Los Angeles advertising campaign ("L.A.'s the place!"), which is repeated in the book, and wanted to know, "The place for what?" Another copy editor working on a manuscript by Pat Rice decided that the heroine wasn't taking the right route into the city and changed it. "Even though," Pat says, "I live here and knew exactly where I was going, and she didn't."

One copy editor wrote a vitriolic letter to the book's editor in which she castigated the author for her appalling sensibility in forcing the Regency heroine to adopt her husband's title after their marriage. The copy editor offered many alternatives that were more "sensitive" and reflected the individuality of the heroine—including a title that would, in fact, imply that the heroine was her husband's sister, and another which was his mother's title! According to the author, "The copy editor was obviously a rabid feminist who had absolutely no concept of British titles and forms of address and clearly thought the author had made them up." As the author points out, it's not *her* fault that Regency England discriminated against women.

Fortunately, her editor was a sensible person who took care of the problem.

On the other hand, sometimes the author *does* just make things up; in a traditional fantasy novel, the author is allowed—nay, expected!—to make up stuff. So I was bewildered to find words and phrases which I had *made up*—which existed nowhere except in my imagination and the manuscript of *In Legend Born*—"corrected" by the copy editor. For example, I would have thought it was obvious that if I referred to a completely fictional ethnic group, one which exists solely in my fantasy world, as the "sea-born folk" more than one hundred times, the copy editor would realize that I *meant* "sea-born folk" and would not feel compelled to change it, every single damn time, to "sea borne folk." Thereby causing me to write "stet" more than one hundred times when I received the copy edit. (Yes, there is a good reason that writers buy stet stamps.)

Of course, sometimes copy editors just don't like the way we write and are, it seems, convinced they can do it better. And so they try. Consequently, Joan Johnston (who couldn't get all the changes changed *back* in a particular book, alas) disclaims all responsibility if you find a soldier "barking" in one of her books. The poor fellow, through no fault of Joan's, also blurts and belches a lot of his dialogue, rather than simply saying it. In a book by another writer, a couple is in the midst of a difficult personal relationship when the hero is suddenly hospitalized after being stabbed. As the heroine looks at his pain-filled face, she reflects on all the important things she should have said to him, and she hopes there's still time to say these things...or rather she *did*, until the copy editor crossed it all out and wrote, "She was upset he'd been hurt." When Susan Mallery wrote that a character was "feeling lower than a snake's fanny pack," the copy editor asked if she was aware that snakes do not wear clothing of any kind. My favorite example, however, is a copy editor who "corrected" a phrase of Susan Wiggs' to "she pulled herself across the room by her teeth." (Is anyone else having a scary mental image now?)

The copy editor of my (by now infamous) *Celestial Bodies* manuscript clearly felt that I wasn't wordy and long-winded enough (though *Kirkus* reviewers have been known to hold the exact opposite view of my work). To give you one example from among many dozens: She altered the phrase "she wanted more than sex from him" to "she wanted more than the feelings of the experience of sex from him." (*Really*, I'm not making this up.) Have I mentioned that I sent a hysterical nine-page letter to my editor about that copy edit? Although it was years ago, I still feel headachy whenever I think about it.

You'll be pleased to know I've saved the best story for last. Bestseller Pat Rice tells of a copy edit that got progressively nastier as she worked her way through the manuscript, with the copy editor virtually snarling at Pat's writing and her characters, going far beyond anything the author had ever before seen a copy editor do to a book. When the copy editor called the heroine "a total ninnyhammer," Pat put down the manuscript and phoned her editor. Her editor looked into the problem, but the copy editor was no longer available for comment...He'd had a nervous breakdown and had been packed off to a psychiatric hospital! (I sincerely hope he was sharing his room there with the copy editor of *Celestial Bodies*.)

Although a good copy editor is worth her weight in chocolate, a bad one makes you jumpy about copy edits for the rest of your career. A good copy editor, like a good editor or agent, is a tremendous asset to a writer. A bad copy editor, like a bad editor or agent, is a huge burden to a poor working writer who doesn't need this kind of senseless aggravation.

("She wanted more than the feelings of the experience of sex from him." I ask you, what kind of person *writes* a phrase like that???)

True Believer

O kay, that does it, I think I'm finally ready to become a lesbian.

Now, I've never had much sympathy for lesbians, because no matter what sort of prejudice they encounter, I continue to believe, from personal experience and lifelong observation, that no one knows the suffering, the frustration, and the hopeless confusion of a heterosexual woman.

If you're a heterosexual woman, you already know what I mean. If you're a man, you never will. And if you're a lesbian, count your blessings, chick.

Anyhow, according to a study done by some research team and then reported on National Public Radio, only about one-third of American men wash their hands after they go to the bathroom.

Even if these statistics are a bit skewed, this somehow seems like the last straw to me. Enough is enough, and I've decided I want to become a lesbian.

This option (lesbianism) might never have occurred to me, except that there've been a lot of lesbians in the entertainment headlines in the past decade. For example, there was the highly-publicized break-up of Hollywood's so-called lesbian power couple, Ellen DeGeneres and Anne Heche. And I must say, the parting of that couple shocked me—and also reminded me of why I write fantasy and romance novels.

Ellen DeGeneres and Anne Heche were so intensely paparazzi'd as a couple that even *I* knew about them. Not until long after everyone else knew about them, of course, but I eventually caught on. Then, while watching TV one night, I happened to catch the final few minutes of an interview with Anne Heche, which was evidently scheduled to promote a soon-to-be-aired cable movie which she and DeGeneres had worked on together. And what Heche said fascinated me.

I didn't know this (and maybe you didn't either), but Heche was heterosexual when she met DeGeneres. She said that she was so taken with this extraordinary person, so utterly and thoroughly convinced that this was the person she was meant to spend the rest of her life with, that the sexuality issue was irrelevant to her. She didn't see a gender (she said), she saw a person and fell in love with that person.

The interview briefly digressed into some stuff about how Heche was stunned that the gender issue seemed to matter to everyone *else* (yeah, right, as if there was ever any doubt the media would gobble up this relationship like it was my mother's bread-pudding); but then the discussion returned to her conviction that she had undergone this complete shift in her sexual identity because Ellen was the love of her life, and they would be together forever.

I admit, I was pretty riveted by that. I even made plans to watch their movie...but that would have required me to actually

locate my cable guide and find out when it was on, and somehow
the effort became too daunting, and I never did it.

However, I did think about Heche's comments several times
thereafter, genuinely moved by the tale she had related. I mean,
isn't this the heart of great love stories—that no obstacle is too
great to overcome when soul mates finally find each other? Juliet
wasn't going to let Romeo's being a Montague stand in the way of
their love. Rhett wasn't going to let Ashley Wilkes, or several hus-
bands, or even the Civil War keep him from having Scarlet. And
Heche wasn't going to let gender interfere with the love of her life.
(I admit, biologically, I was baffled by that; but philosophically, I
found it enthralling.)

Isn't what Heche described, in fact, the very essence of
what romance writers explore in their novels? Characters who
must confront problems, make choices, and enact changes in
their external and their internal lives in order to accommodate
the most important opportunity and fulfilling experience of their
lives—namely, finding true love? And aren't Heche and DeGeneres (I thought to myself) also *who* romance writers write about?
Not mundane "this person will make a comfortable spouse, so
let's get married" couples, but passionate "I'll move mountains,
make sacrifices, and pursue this with relentless courage, because
nothing else matters as much as this love" couples.

Right there, in this celebrity couple whom I had always
ignored, was precisely such a grand, passionate, and gutsy love
story. I mean, talk about a strong internal and external conflict!
Being a straight person who suddenly falls powerfully and
irrevocably in love with someone of your own gender! Wow. I,
who have plotted numerous love stories in two genres, had never
thought of that conflict—and it's a powerful one, particularly

given social ramifications which are at least as daunting as the more traditional conflicts of (for example) "my soul mate is my blood enemy" or "my soul mate is of a different social class."

Although it didn't seem to be a big deal to Heche when she gave that interview, *I* thought it was a tremendous testimony to love that, upon meeting the soul mate whose gender didn't coincide with her heterosexuality, this woman changed her sexual identity. I thought it represented enormous courage, precisely the kind that romance protagonists are supposed to discover in themselves, that she chose to defy public opinion in favor of being true to her heart, in all its rich capacity and surprising horizons.

I thought this was really cool.

Okay, yeah, I also knew there could be more to it (or less to it) than that; but one of the skills you develop as a writer is to know when to leave the story alone, to recognize when it's j-u-s-t right. And the story I was left with after that interview was just right.

So I was disappointed—yes, even shocked—when DeGeneres and Heche split up only a few months later. This enormous, life-altering love had lasted...not even four years? I have a forty-dollar pair of sandals that's lasted longer than that. Doesn't it seem like the love of one's life, the soul mate for whom one changed one's sexual identity, the person whom one was destined to be with forever...Doesn't it seem like that should last longer than a decent pair of sandals?

Well, what do I know about these people? Maybe their highly public lives created problems and pressures which even a great love couldn't withstand. Or maybe it wasn't such a great love, after all. Maybe it was a pretty typical affair, even a mundane one, romanticized by its participants for the benefit of the press. I have no idea.

I just believe in enduring love, and I like to see it confirmed from time to time. That's not the romance writer in me. That's *me*—and that *me* is what makes it possible for me to be a good romance writer.

I also believe in (and occasionally need reassuring confirmation of) terrible courage, passionate commitment, and unassailable loyalty. I need to believe in sacrifice and redemption, in the heroic inside of each of us, in the cause for which it is worth dying, in the love for which it is worth living, in the war worth fighting, and in the peace worth sacrificing for. Needing to believe in these things is what makes me a good fantasy writer.

I need to believe in all of this, yet I am daily confronted with a world where half of all marriages end in divorce, where wars are complex economic endeavors bearing no relation to the noble ideals so cynically used to promote them to the taxpaying public, and where people often say "I love you" merely to grease the wheels rather than as an expression of profound commitment.

I'd like to believe that there are occasionally national leaders who are moral and brave, who fight for ideals and fearlessly oppose wrong-doers (no matter *how* big the campaign contribution was). I want to believe there are religious leaders whose lives evoke the essence of the faiths they profess. I need to believe that a good person reaps the karma of good deeds, and that a bad person gets what's coming to her. Above all, I need to believe that the world is a mysterious, surprising, magical, glamorous, heart-wrenching, tragic, glorious, wildly amusing place where anything can happen.

Which is what's wonderful and, I now realize, genuinely important about popular fiction. It's written by believers for believers about believers. It reaffirms that it's okay for me to need to believe in the things I need to believe in, and it assures me that other people out there need to believe in them, too—despite the daily assaults that the real world launches against these beliefs.

When you pick up a romance novel, you know that *these* lovers really will make an enduring commitment. When you open a mystery novel, you can count on the detective bringing the killer to justice; and you know the killer won't become the darling of the talk show circuit after getting off on a technicality. The reader of a fantasy novel can count on good ultimately triumphing over evil, whatever the cost, because true heroism is inherently stronger and more enduring than villainy.

Popular fiction is like a homeopathic treatment of the soul. As long as you keep verifying for yourself that lasting love, true courage, and real justice do indeed exist, you can prevent the ignominy, which also exists, from taking over your system and making you toxic. The petty, the mundane, and the disappointing in our world have been recorded since mankind first began writing; fortunately, though, so have the basic themes of heroism, justice, and love which are, in our era, still affirmed in the pages of popular fiction.

So it's a pretty worthwhile profession we have, a constant vocation to assure true believers that fleeting love, petty cowardice, and miscarriages of justice are not (despite appearances to the contrary) the standards by which we should measure ourselves, others, or the world we live in. Our standards should always be high, because no matter how distant the stars we reach for, they are attainable. I, as a popular fiction novelist, imagine this, and it's my job to make others believe whatever I imagine.

Now, if I could just believe that the next attractive man whom I meet always washes his hands after going to the bathroom...

...Does Not Meet Our Needs At This Time...

Let's talk about rejection.

For those of you who've either never heard this before or who've heard it but didn't really believe it, let me state a fact that never fails to startle some people: Professional writers get rejected. All of the time. Even by their own publishers. Even by editors who like them personally and like their writing. In fact, *multi-published, award-winning writers* get rejected all of the time. Want a real surprise? Even *New York Times* bestsellers still get rejected (though not all of the time, to be sure).

Rejection is not the unique burden of the aspiring writer; it is a common way of life for the *professional* writer. Receiving dozens of rejection letters as an aspiring writer is just preparing you for life as a professional one.

As I've mentioned before, *New York Times* bestselling science fiction/fantasy author Kevin J. Anderson, who has over fifteen million copies of his books in print, has a collection of 800 rejection slips—only about ten percent of which he received *before* making his first sale. A mega-star of the romance genre once told me it took her several years to sell the novel that became her first *New York Times* bestseller, even though she was a published romance novelist while she was submitting it and getting rejected. A current women's fiction bestseller found her first "breakout" book rejected all over New York before it found the right home, though she was a multi-published novelist at the time.

I sold the first two novels I ever wrote…but then four of the next six books I submitted were rejected. In addition, between my tenth and eleventh book sales to romance publisher Silhouette Books, my editor rejected four proposals in a row.

My thirteenth published romance novel, *Fever Dreams* (written under my romance pseudonym, Laura Leone), was rejected by my own then-publisher, then rejected by several other publishers before I finally found a buyer for it. I made my first science fiction/fantasy deal only *after* my first two sf/f submissions were rejected by every editor in the free world.

Getting rejections as a published writer is discouraging and depressing. (If you don't believe me, just ask around.) Some people have blustering confidence and unshakable faith in themselves; but most of us, after a project is rejected several times, start to fear that we'll never sell again. One busy writer, after getting several rejections, said to me in all seriousness, "I think maybe I was just an eighteen-book fluke."

Professional writers get rejected precisely because editors don't buy books they don't like, don't want, aren't enthused about, or don't think they can market successfully. Just because an author has sold books somewhere before is no reason for an editor to say, "Gosh, I guess I'll buy this book even though I don't like it and don't expect readers to buy it." Nor does an editor buy a book like that just because the author has sold books specifically to *her* before, or has won awards, or is a pal—or for any other reason. This is a business, and an editor only buys a book if she thinks it's a good business decision.

For example, if you're the extremely successful author of a dozen elegant historical romances and you suddenly write a lesbian-terrorist-nun romance set in modern Nigeria, there's a strong possibility that your editor will refuse to buy it.

Okay, so that was an easy example. Here's a trickier one: If you're that same author and you submit your thirteenth elegant historical romance...your editor may still reject it. She may think it's not up to your usual standards and therefore won't help sales, or she may think that there's some aspect of it that will actively hurt sales.

Speaking of sales, here's another reason the editor may reject that book: Your sales figures have flattened out, or even dropped, and the publisher has decided you're not profitable enough, no matter how good a writer you are. So they dump you. Even if the editor loves the proposal for that thirteenth book, she won't buy it if the publisher has decided that continuing the relationship with you would be a bad business decision.

Yes, all of these examples happen. Relatively often, in fact.

However, most rejections aren't *disastrous* by any means. In general, they're just par for the course, the cost of doing business, the inevitable risks a writer lives with every day of her career.

I would describe a "disaster," instead, as a book that gets rejected after it's *under contract*. Once the work is under contract, you feel like you've dodged the rejection bullet and, whatever else happens, at least the book is sold and will be released. So when you finish writing the book and deliver that under-contract manuscript, it's a real blow when the editor tells you the book is awful, and she won't accept it. It's not only a terrible blow to your confidence and your release schedule, it's also a hideous blow to your finances. You deliver a book thinking that you'll be paid the second installment of your advance after the editor reads the manuscript. However, if she doesn't accept it, you don't get paid. And, in many cases, you therefore can't pay your bills.

Yes, this happens. More often than some people realize, since it's usually kept pretty quiet. Writers tell their friends, but they certainly don't make public announcements about it. No one benefits from publicizing that their own editor thinks their latest manuscript is so bad that it's actually unpublishable.

Publishing contracts specify a process that must then take place. Usually, the publisher can ask for "reasonable revisions"—which is very vague, indeed, as legal terms go!

For example, the editor may say, "This is utterly unsalvageable, and I see no way of fixing it, nor can I bear the thought of having to read any version of it ever again. Please burn it, and write a completely different book." That usually means there is little hope of resolving the impasse, though I've known writers who have nonetheless tried to revise the book under such circumstances. (I do not, however, personally know of anyone whose editor then did an about-face and accepted it—though I do know of at least one case where the editor left and the editor who replaced her accepted the book.)

But, again, let's try a less extreme example: The editorial request for revisions may be more "reasonable" than suggesting you use the manuscript to start a bonfire, but the author may

nonetheless feel she cannot "reasonably" agree, because it's
obvious that her vision of the novel differs too much from the
editor's vision for this ever to work out to anyone's satisfaction. In that case, the author may try to accommodate the
editor, or the two of them may just argue about their differing
visions for a few months.

In any event, at a certain point, the author becomes legally
free to market the book elsewhere. Many contracts specifically
provide for this contingency, spelling out when or under what
circumstances the author (a) can sell elsewhere and (b) would
be obliged to repay the signing advance that the original
publisher paid her. One way to avoid repaying the money (and
to attempt to salvage the publishing relationship) is to write
a replacement book, a novel which the publisher does accept
in place of the refused novel. I know of at least one instance
where this not only worked, but led to a long-term, amicable,
and lucrative relationship between author and publisher.

Such contingencies are covered in contracts precisely
because writers *do* turn in manuscripts that editors declare
"unacceptable" and refuse to pay for or to publish. The good
news is that writers often do sell those books elsewhere. No,
not always; but I do know of many cases where they have done
so. For example, a science fiction writer received a Nebula
nomination for a novel that he'd taken elsewhere after the
original publisher declared it unacceptable.

So whether or not a book is publishable is often a wholly
subjective opinion. However, even if the editor is wrong, the
"unacceptable" book is indeed publishable, and it eventually
sells elsewhere, the writer meanwhile endures disastrous

financial consequences imposed by the editor's bad judgment call and the publisher's support of it.

Yet while your bills mount up and your bank account dwindles to a big fat zero, the editor and everyone else at the publishing house is still getting paid a regular salary. And it's truly remarkable how many of them don't understand that *not* getting paid is actually a problem for writers, go figure.

Resolutions

As the cold days and long nights of winter settle into my bloodstream and produce a sleepy, apathetic effect not unlike my reaction to reading Victorian literature, I take this opportunity to review my New Year's resolutions. Being thrifty by nature, I tend to use many of the same ones every year, thus cutting down on the amount of thought I have to invest in them.

1. Resolved: I will invest more thought in things.
   Oops.

2. Resolved: I will eat right.
   This one didn't go so well last year. (Or the year before that, or the year before that, or the year before that, etc.) By mid-year, I was on first-name terms with all the lads at the new pizza delivery place, and my chocolate consumption had a perceptible effect on the worldwide economy.

3. Resolved: I will exercise regularly.

I was such a total stranger at the local yoga school this past year that I was stunned to discover it had doubled its size, changed its class schedule, completely remodeled its interior, and shifted the location of its lobby between the day I first joined it and the day when I finally showed up to take a class.

On the other hand, I did start tai chi lessons—only six years after first deciding to do so. And what good timing! Classes began soon after my publisher suddenly decided to spend several weeks torturing me to the best of its ability—and we all know how good publishers are at that. What a relief it was, after a day of being repeatedly poked in the eye with sharp sticks (so to speak), to go to class, with soothing pseudo-Chinese music playing softly on the stereo, and lose myself in the moment. (In addition to which, I look really *cool* doing tai chi.)

4. Resolved: I will wear clean clothes every day.

Isn't it good that I've still got a realistic goal to pursue from scratch in the New Year?

5. Resolved: I will deliver my work weeks early.

Okay, I only keep this resolution on the annual list as a nostalgic reminder of how young, energetic, and foolishly optimistic I once was.

6. Resolved: I will meet all deadlines.

This resolution has become ambivalent over the years.

The first time I ever missed a deadline was way back in my early days as a Silhouette writer, when I phoned my editor to warn her I'd be delivering a book two weeks late. At the time,

I was consumed with guilt and a burning sense of inadequacy over such behavior.

That's only because I was so inexperienced.

An editor once told me that a colleague asked her why she had such a high proportion of writers who delivered on time, compared to the colleague's own list of many late-deliverers. She explained that it was because her writers responded to her own behavior: She read manuscripts soon after delivery, authorized payment quickly, and edited books within a reasonable period of time. While such measures may sound to a novice like the minimum prerequisites of a competent editor, any writer who's been in the business for a decade knows how special such behavior actually is.

I myself have waited up to five months for a signing check, thirteen months for an edit, six months for a delivery check, and twenty-seven months for publication. Your mileage may vary, but I certainly know from the complaints and anecdotes of my friends and acquaintances that this kind of treatment is all too common. One writer I know was heavily pressured by both editor and agent to deliver a manuscript by a certain date...and then it sat around for over half a year with no editing. Another writer's editor still hadn't even given her manuscript a first read (let alone a delivery payment) six months after delivery.

Given enough experiences like this, the staunch sense of professional obligation to meet those deadlines can eventually (go figure) get a little weak. A writer's self-respect may well stop being defined by meeting deadlines if no one she deals with seems to be on any more specific a schedule than "I'll get around it to eventually."

I'm not saying that lowering our professional standards

as writers is right or good. Please note, I still put "I will meet all deadlines" on my New Year's Resolutions list every year. Despite my exasperation with a profession sheltering editors who treat delivered manuscripts with all the urgency I normally reserve for dusting the basement, I nonetheless fully intend to—and make every effort to—meet my deadlines. I don't always succeed (and, on occasion, my lateness is truly epic), but I always try. I make this effort because meeting deadlines honors the standards I set for myself as a professional. And also because, frankly, meeting deadlines places me on the moral high ground, and I like the view.

Nonetheless, while striving to meet all my deadlines this year, I'll keep in mind the words one editor wrote to me last year: "You're not the first writer to be late, and if all of them delivered such terrific final results as this, I'd be tickled pink."

7. Resolved: I will eschew envy.

Writers drive themselves crazy with envy all of the time. You know: "Why do her semi-literate books sell ten times better than mine do?" or, "We started out at exactly the same time, but now he makes double the money I do," or, "We have the same editor and write in the same subgenre and *I* get better reviews, so why does *she* get five times the promotional support that I do?"

Envy is most seductive when it seems justified: *I* am the better writer, *I* am the nicer person, *I* have worked harder, *I* have been publishing longer, I do better research, I *deserve* more success than they do!

But envy is always poisonous. *Always.* It always hurts me far more than it hurts whomever I'm envying. It gains me nothing, and it costs me far too much: peace of mind, focus, energy, contentment, self-worth, self-respect, good digestion, sound sleep, and—need I even add?—personal charm.

So I vow that every time I feel the poison of envy seep into my blood, I will try to flush it out. Luckily, my local ice cream shop makes a chocolate shake that really helps with this. (So there's a valid reason, you see, that I have trouble with Resolution 2.)

8. Resolved: I will not compare myself to others.

Nursing a sense of inadequacy is no more productive than harboring envy. If someone writes faster than I, gets up earlier, has a smaller waistline, understands the business better, keeps her office tidier, does more research in less time, and always has a sunny disposition...

Well, actually, yes, that's *plenty* of reason for me to feel inadequate by comparison.

But I vow not to do so. That person has her own inadequacies, even if they're not immediately apparent to me; after all, *my* inadequacies aren't always immediately apparent to everyone I meet. The beauty of this profession is that it's so individualistic. As long as I work toward being the best writing professional *I* can be, I'm doing my job. And my job isn't going to get any easier if I worry about how you're doing yours.

9. Resolved: I will not let the bastards get me down.

This is a tough one. Especially because the definition of "the bastards" for a writer can be a lot like the definition of "parasites" if you're a mammal in tropical Africa. I mean, wow, there are so many possibilities that I sometimes find myself paralyzed just by the sheer volume of life forms lining up to eat my eyeballs or infest my liver.

(Sorry about the imagery.)

One of my publishers spent last autumn torturing me. Each time I thought that surely they had finally run out of possible ways to screw up my professional life, they came up with yet another innovation. Things got so bad that, at one point, I instructed my agent to pull everything that was under contract there. I decided I'd actually rather never publish again than keep working under those circumstances. I meant it. I still mean it. The camel's back broke, Elvis left the building, the temple of the Philistines came crashing down.

Go on, tell me *you're* so Zen-enlightened serene that this crap never gets you down. I dare you.

As it happens, my agent managed to resolve that particular mess in my favor, so all's well that ends well. Apart from, oh, the insomnia, the digestive disorders, and the tension headaches that dominated that entire season.

Three of my friends were dumped by their publishers around that time. At least two of them were working with editors whom I frankly think should be locked in a room with old disco albums for the rest of their lives. Another friend spent part of the year having agent-from-hell adventures.

Been there. Done that. Compiling a list of suitable LPs.

Internet piracy. Plagiarism. Hate mail. Ugly *Kirkus* reviews and snide *Publishers Weekly* reviews. Vicious Amazon reader reviews and really strange cover copy. Shipping mistakes, distribution disasters, art department gaffs, and printer errors. Spiraling sales figures, the midlist crunch, disappearing markets, rising costs, and vanishing retail outlets.

Oh, man, I'm making myself depressed.

But, despite all the reasons there are for a working writer

to feel really, really down, here's what I don't like about giving into it: It lets the bastards win. It gives them too much power. Besides that, depression makes it hard to write.

10. Resolved: I will count my blessings.

The truth is, the bastards *do* get me down. So I have to pick myself up. I have a real dread of becoming an embittered troll surrounded by a dark cloud of venomous gloom—and I certainly picked the wrong profession if I wanted to make sure I could definitely never wind up like *that*. So I vow, once again, to combat the forces of darkness (i.e. almost everything that occurs to me on a daily basis in the publishing world) by regularly remembering to focus on all the reasons I have, as a writer, to thank the universe.

I have my health. And I know there are people whose health affects their ability to write.

I have great and cherished friends in this business. Their value is above rubies, and I wouldn't have missed knowing them for the world.

I have the opportunity to meet many writers whom I read. I even have the opportunity to read many writers whom I meet.

I'm a multi-published novelist, in a world where most people will only ever dream of selling even one novel.

I mostly get to write only what I want to write. Although I have written some things just because I needed the money, I haven't had to do it very often or very recently.

In a tough market where many good writers are currently unable to get contracts or are getting offers with bad terms, I'm under contract and happy with the terms.

Though I certainly have a love-hate relationship with my

work, I nonetheless find it artistically challenging, exciting, and satisfying, and it has so far been professionally rewarding for me.

I am often struck by how many people hate their jobs, or at least are indifferent to their professions. You know: "It's okay," or, "It's a living," or, "I like parts of it," or, "It's better than digging ditches." Writing, however, is an obsession and a way of life. And no matter how the bastards get me down, aren't I LUCKY to have such a driving passion in my professional life! Aren't I LUCKY to do something for a living that I'd probably be doing for free if I hadn't been able to turn it into my profession! I count it as a blessing that, despite the frustration and despair that my profession regularly inflicts on me, I am not going through my professional life only half-alive, the way so many people in this world do.

Finally, I count as a blessing that, on a regular basis, I get to force my opinions on *you*.

The Best Bad Advice

S o a friend of mine, a professional actress, is at lunch one
day with several old school chums. None of them are
actors, nor even remotely connected to the business. They
know nothing whatsoever about the working life of an actor,
but they're nonetheless full of unsolicited advice. When my
friend admits that she's gone to a lot of auditions but hasn't
gotten a role in months, they come up with a brilliant plan:
"I know! Why don't you go work in *films* for a while? Once
you've become successful there, wouldn't it be easier to get
stage jobs?"

Well, yes. It probably would. That's true.

It's also true that once you've become a successful film
actor, it's probably easier to run for political office, beat felony
charges, get invited to the White House, meet supermodels and
star athletes, get your picture on magazine covers, and land a
huge advance for a book.

Wait a minute...Land a huge advance for a book?

Wow! Why didn't *I* think of that? If I had just starred in

a few films first, maybe I wouldn't have had to serve my tour of duty in the underpaid and overcrowded trenches of midlist fiction. Damn! How absentminded of me.

Where was this advice when I needed it?

Oh, wait. Now I remember. It was in the same boat with advice like: "I know! Why don't you sell a movie script and make a million dollars?" Or better yet: "Why don't you write my idea, and after you sell it, I'll split the money with you?" And my personal favorite: "Why don't you write my life story, and after you sell it, I'll split the money with you?"

An acquaintance once wondered why I don't just deliberately write a bestseller and thereby secure my financial freedom.

I'll give you three guesses on this one:

(a) I'm too fine and noble to lower myself to writing a bestseller.

(b) I think it would be morally wrong to get a seven-figure advance before putting in two or three decades of hard work as a midlist novelist.

(c) I've yet to write a novel that any publisher wanted to buy for that kind of money. Nor have any of my books turned into word-of-mouth runaway bestsellers in astonishing defiance of my publishers' expectations.

If you guessed (a) or (b), then I suggest you go star in some films for a while.

As my friend, the actress, noted after her luncheon with her eagerly helpful old school chums, she had been trying to get a film *audition* ever since leaving drama school. And unless you're a celebrity (or providing extremely intimate services to the right person), you usually have to get a film audition before you can get a film role—let alone enough significant film roles that theatrical producers fall all over themselves to give you a job when you decide you want to perform on the stage.

Meanwhile—barring the shortcut of becoming a movie star first, of course—the way to get a seven-figure advance in our business is to write a novel that some publisher thinks hundreds of thousands of people will choose to buy (in hardcover) when it's released. And in order to write a word-of-mouth runaway bestseller, you have to write a novel that hundreds of thousands of people decide to buy even though the publisher, not expecting this, didn't promote the book (or even give it a large enough initial print run).

Pop quiz. I have never written a novel that sold for a seven-figure advance or went into a tenth printing because:

(a) I'm too fine and noble to write down the surefire million-dollar book ideas that plague me day and night.
(b) I feel it would be unfair to the rest of you.
(c) Life doesn't love me that much yet.

If you guessed **(a)** or **(b)**, then you should go call Tom Hanks and offer to co-star in his next movie.

I'm always baffled by well-meaning advice like, "Gosh, I have a suggestion! Why don't you just soar overnight to the pinnacle of your profession?" In the many years that I've been a professional writer, I have never once told a doctor, lawyer, or Indian chief how to achieve overnight success in *their* vocations. I've never told them how to run their careers or do their jobs. I have always assumed that they, full-time professionals in those fields, know far more about them than I do. Yet an astonishing number of people who know nothing about the publishing business nonetheless seem to assume that they know more about my profession than I do and therefore feel obliged to advise me about it.

I'm occasionally pinned into a corner by people who don't even *read* fiction (never mind reading *my* fiction), but who insist on telling me what I should write if I want to sell books (sort of ignoring the fact that I *already* sell books). I could quit writing for a living if I had a dollar for every person who, while knowing nothing whatsoever about our business, has offered me business advice. I've also been told quite emphatically, any number of times, that I shouldn't spend my own money to go to big national conventions like the World Science Fiction Convention. No, I should "make" my publisher pay my way to such events, or else refuse to go. (Every time someone gives me this advice, I picture the incredulous guffaws in New York which would greet such a demand.) My explanation that it is I, not my publisher, who benefits from my attendance at such events, because I'm a freelancer who goes there to make useful contacts, promote my name, and keep abreast of my industry, usually gets brushed aside as an irrelevant comment made by someone who hasn't thought this through clearly.

However, as tiresome as this sort of thing may be, at least I know it's not happening because something about my face says to people, "I'm an idiot, and I desperately desire professional advice offered from a standpoint of total ignorance." Before you start making wisecracks about what my face says to *you*, I hasten to point out that almost every writer I know endures unsolicited advice from people who don't know what they're talking about, but who offer it up because...What? The publishing business is child's play? The answers to writers' career problems are inside fortune cookies? Oprah did a show on it?

Or maybe because writing is one of those professions, like acting, that so many people have fantasized about or thought they could do successfully—someday, in their spare time—and we writers (and actors) are just destined to keep bumping into these people for the rest of our lives.

Anyhow, it's not just me. A friend of mine returns from extended family gatherings several times a year, grinding her teeth over the emphatic and wholly unrequested advice she has received about what to write and how to run her career. Another friend had a colleague at her day job who regularly inflicted unwanted guidance upon her. This included telling her she must copyright every story before submitting it, or publishers would steal it. He also advised her never to use paperclips in her submissions because (wait for it!) publishers "keep them and make a good income from them." (Yes, I'm still trying to figure out that one.)

"You should try writing short stories first. They're easier!" was a piece of advice that regularly plagued Maggie Shayne when she was an aspiring novelist, along with: "You should try writing children's stories. They're easier!" Gosh, if only Maggie had listened to that advice...Oh, wait, if she had listened to that advice, then today she wouldn't be an award-winning romance writer with more than thirty published novels to her credit.

When writer Janni Lee Simner was first starting out, any number of people told her she'd never sell a story because "you don't know anybody in publishing, after all." When novelist Lillian Stewart Carl introduced herself at the counter of a bookstore, the bookseller told her she needed to get on *Oprah* first if she wanted to sell a book (sort of ignoring the fact that she *already* sold books). Because, presumably, getting on *Oprah* is your next best choice if you can't manage to become a movie star before writing a novel.

Bestselling fantasy novelist Raymond E. Feist was once a guest speaker at a writing class where he heard the instructor give them one of my favorite pieces of bad advice: "Don't worry about spelling or punctuation or style. If the editor really likes the story, he'll find someone to fix all that stuff for you." Yes, and if the NBA really likes your height, they'll find someone else to do all the shooting, dribbling, and passing for you. (I am always amazed at just how many people tell aspiring writers—*writers*, for God's sake!—that spelling, punctuation, and grammar don't matter and won't affect their chances of selling their work professionally.)

The piece of bad advice that full-time writer Steve Perry best remembers was some long-ago creative writing teacher who assured him that he could never make a living as a writer or quit his day job. (So Steve and all the full-time writers I know are evidently figments of my imagination. Come to think of it, that must mean *I'm* a figment of my imagination. This could be handy at tax time.) Of course, "you'll never make a living" is a very common warning to fiction writers—and even more common to poets. Someone once told Jane Yolen, "Your poetry is wonderful, but don't try to make a living that way." Yolen describes it as some of the most useless and counterproductive advice she ever got, adding, "I now make plenty of money on my children's poetry, thank you."

However, the worst bad advice surely comes from people actually *in* the business, since it carries a dangerous air of credibility with it. Raymond Feist recalls once hearing an editor tell an audience that he preferred first-time writers to approach him directly, *not* through an agent. Feist says, "Under my breath I muttered, 'And armies prefer it when the other guys surrender without firing a shot.'" George R.R. Martin says the worst advice he ever got was also from an editor, one who'd been fired and replaced by someone new. The dismissed editor told Martin what to say to "break the ice" with the new editor over lunch. Martin followed the advice. The result: "It was the worst lunch I ever had in this business." Not only did he never sell a word to the new editor, but when the lunch check came, the editor figured out Martin's share.

Final exam. When do you take advice about your writing career?

(a) When your brother-in-law gives it.

(b) When a stranger gives it.

(c) When you've double-checked the source, triple-checked the facts, and thoroughly considered how well the advice in question applies to you, your work, your goals, and your specific situation.

If you answered (a) or (b), it's time for you to go nudge Brad Pitt and Julia Roberts out of the limelight.

Enlarge Your Penis

I wake up. I tumble out of bed. I throw cold water on my face. I make coffee. (And, no, I do not intend to give up the vice of caffeine, not ever, so don't even start with me.) I search for my slippers. I can't find them. I search for my glasses, so I'll have a better chance of finding my slippers. I wander into my office. I look at my work. My work looks at me. I sit down at the computer and check my e-mail. It says:

ENLARGE YOUR PENIS!

I ask you, is this the sort of thing anyone—I mean, even someone who *has* a penis—really wants to read first thing in the morning?

INCEST! SEE DAUGHTER AND DAD GO AT IT!

I feel queasy. I delete the penis and incest e-mails without opening them. I scroll further down the list of messages in my e-mailbox.

KEEP HER HAPPY WITH VIAGRA!

Once and for all, I do not have a penis! Get a clue! Get a life! Get out of my mailbox!

GIRLS HAVING SEX WITH DOGS AND HORSES!

Thanks for *that* mental image which I will now spend the rest of the morning trying to shed.

In fact, since I was raised at a dog kennel (yes, really), I actually know quite a bit about how dogs have sex. It's physiologically so different from how people have sex that, involuntarily, I start wondering about the technical aspects of how a girl and a... No! No! I do not want to be thinking about this! Stop it! Stop it *now*.

Ah, the information age. How the Internet has changed our drab little lives.

MAKE ME WET.

Sorry, I've got a deadline to meet just now.

EARN $80,000 AT HOME IN YOUR SPARE TIME!

Better.

DEBT-RIDDEN? DESPERATE? LET ME HELP!

I suppose it's a sign of the times that financial "spam" is now just as ubiquitous as porn spam. Every day, when I open my e-mailbox, I am promised the chance to make a fortune at home in my spare time with no skills, I am offered investment advice and opportunities, and I am presented with solutions to debt. Wow. What an exciting life of low-risk, substantial-return opportunities I lead while waiting for the coffee to finish brewing each morning.

As a novelist, I applaud creativity. So I was rather impressed upon receiving an e-mail from Nigerian Brigadier-General Bibiola Waritimi proposing a scheme for our mutual profit. (Hey, it beats getting yet another e-mail inviting me to SEE CHEERLEADERS BOFFING WARTHOGS!!) He informs me that he confiscated fifty million dollars from a Liberian warlord during an international peacekeeping operation in

West Africa. He explains that he now needs an honest partner in the United States—someone just like me, in fact!—to help him transfer the money to an American bank. My reward for assisting him in this entirely legal and foolproof process will be about fifteen million dollars. Gosh, is this guy the answer to an exhausted novelist's prayers or *what*?

(The Nigerian Letter Scam is so classic that it's described in detail in private investigator Fay Faron's *Rip-Off: A Writer's Guide to Crimes of Deception*, published in 1998 by Writer's Digest Books.)

My personal favorite, though, is an e-mail that does not offer me either money or sex with barnyard animals, but which instead begins: "If you are a time traveler or alien, and in possession of alien or government technology, I need your help!"

Come on, could you really resist reading the rest of a spam letter that begins like that?

The correspondent explains that he is cursed, dying, in danger, and suffering. (In other words, a *very* bad hair day.) He needs to travel back in time to solve his problems, and he's looking for sophisticated technical help. (So, of course, he came to me—someone who has yet to master operating a digital alarm clock.) He wants advice on creating a vortex generator, and he also wants to know where to get some glowing, blue moon crystals.

Well, don't we all, buddy?

Which is not to say that the Internet has brought *only* crazies and whackos into my humble home. In fact, in most ways, the Internet is such a great convenience that I'm baffled by people who refuse to log on. I keep in touch with friends and relatives all over the world (yes, even friends in Nigeria) on a regular basis now without racking up huge phone bills or spending a fortune on postage. I can ask people questions in the middle of the night when insomnia attacks, and get a detailed reply at their convenience. I can inform a dozen people at once of something they need to know, and personal news can reach me quickly from the source rather than traveling through a series of people before I finally get the garbled third-hand account.

And I can research almost anything without leaving my office. This is key, since leaving home requires me to swap my slippers for a pair of shoes, and finding my shoes can be an involved process. Especially if I've yet to find my glasses.

You can research *anything* on the Web, no matter how specific, specialized, or obscure it is. Did you know, for example, there's a Congolese rebel group with their own website? A tribe of pygmies with their own website? An e-list for people who are fans of both *Buffy the Vampire Slayer* and novelist Dorothy Dunnett? Whether I want articles about the Nazi plunder of European art during WWII, a weather prediction for tomorrow in Vladivostok, the date and day of Easter in 1527, or a current rate for converting US dollars into Zambian kwacha, I can find it while sitting right here at my keyboard.

When I wanted to know how a private investigator in my novel might legally transport a gun on an international flight, I found the answer on an electronic Bulletin Board (BB) for airline professionals. When I was asked to write a last-minute science fiction/fantasy short story about the Vietnam Memorial Wall, a subject about which I knew nothing, I found all the information I needed on the Web in the middle of the night. When I was researching male prostitutes for my novel *Fallen From Grace*, I not only found websites detailing their services and prices, but also BBs on which some of them chat with prospective clients. For research into a vaguely remembered and truly bizarre incident in my hometown upon which I may one day base a story, all I had to do was tap into the Internet to find newspaper articles twenty years old via my public library's online services.

So—Nigerian swindles and incestuous bestiality notwithstanding—I love the Internet.

VOLUPTUOUS TEENS—RAW!

Well, okay, it's a love-hate relationship.

And, of course, I waste time on the Internet. Way, way too much time.

I chat on e-lists. For example, I belong to an e-list comprised solely of people who were once members of the theatre club at my university. I used to belong to an e-list for fans of the South African rock band, Savuka, but I couldn't keep up with the lengthy political debates there. I even founded an e-list, now 140-people strong, of professional women science fiction/fantasy writers (where we bitch about—wait for it!—publishers, agents, reviewers, and the IRS).

RESNICK AS PREDICTABLE AS EVER!

I also browse newsgroups. Until the TV show *La Femme Nikita* was cancelled, there was a great Usenet newsgroup of *LFN* fans who were articulate and interesting people. (Proof of this description: Some of them read my work.) I legitimized this time expenditure by occasionally asking them research questions, some of which they could actually answer. I also sometimes browse a screenwriters newsgroup, where they mostly give advice-born-out-of-bitter-experience about driving and parking in L.A.

Additionally, I read a lot of obscure online articles which I cannot always truthfully classify as "research." Including articles about Nigeria, where a man has been living in a tree for years. His wife—mother of his nine children—says she doesn't mind bringing him his meals there, but she laments that they haven't had sex in years. One winter, I followed a whole series of online articles and editorials about the escaped cow hiding right outside my apartment. (She staged a daring escape from a slaughterhouse, and the cops spent more than ten days tracking her in my urban neighborhood with no success. At one point, they donned guerilla warfare garb and hid out in the local park for days, where they stationed hollow decoy cows in the hope of attracting her. By the time she was finally caught, she was such a pop-culture heroine that celebrities were bidding on her. A New York artist eventually acquired her as a pet and retired her to a bucolic farm—which, if I understood correctly, is a haven specifically for cows who've made daring escapes from slaughterhouses. But I digress.)

Sadly, I even waste time online arguing with people I don't know about things that probably don't matter. I also bitch with people I trust about things I probably can't change—which may be useless, but at least it's cathartic.

One of my favorite hobbies since entering the information age is following one hyperlink to another to another to another, just out of curiosity, until what begins as a search for a Russian cookbook leads me to browsing the website of a Congolese rebel group. Or perhaps what begins as a search for a website featuring discount airfares winds up with me browsing an online bookstore for an out-of-print tome about nineteenth century French art.

JUST CLICK HERE TO BUY NOW!

Yes, I waste time shopping online. Often for things I have no intention whatsoever of buying. Such as a café in Nova Scotia (I was just curious about what it would cost), or a weekend at a private villa with a male "escort" (I was even *more* curious about what it would cost), or a cello (maybe I'll take lessons some day), or all the books I keep adding to my wish list.

I also lurk on BBs. And, yes, okay, sometimes I post messages there. On one occasion, even though I know better (I know better! I do!), I got absorbed in a passionate, nonsensical, and extremely lengthy debate on one of the BBs of the Science Fiction Writers of America (SFWA). Inexplicably, I had forgotten Resnick's First Rule of Survival: *Never* get involved in a SFWA debate.

SEE INTERNET MADNESS SEIZE NOVELIST!

I like to cook, and my hard drive must now contain six hundred recipes I've downloaded on the off-chance that I'll suddenly feel compelled to make Boeuf Wellington and Baked Alaska for twenty. I love to travel, and I've bookmarked nearly forty alternative travel sites, so that I'll be ready to act the moment it's time to book an Amazon jungle trek or run off to teach English in Mongolia. Because one should always have such choices at one's fingertips, in case six months and several thousand dollars should suddenly make themselves available without advance notice.

But to return to enlarged penises...

After I established a website (www.LauraResnick.com), I was pleased to discover that, contrary to the emphatic claims of every publisher I've ever written for, I actually do have readers. Not only do they log onto my website, they even leave nice messages in my guestbook. Unfortunately, so do giddy purveyors of enlarged penises, i.e. porn merchants. Since I am too cheap to pay my webmaster to do it, about once a month I have to log into my guestbook and use my password to delete messages left there inviting my readers to see naked, two-headed gymnasts kissing donkeys, or whatever.

Still, it could be worse. Some porn merchant managed to hack into novelist Edith Layton's website and give it new programming, so that every time a reader clicked her guestbook link, they were instantly transported to a German porn site. As Edith says, "The thought of my romance readers finding themselves eyeing naked frolicking Fräuleins instead of my circumspect heroines still appalls me."

One of the coolest things about all Internet activity is that it's great camouflage. You're sitting at your keyboard staring intently at your computer screen, moving your mouse, and often typing. What could look more like *work*?

Of course, the actual amount of work I'm getting done is not increasing along with the amount of time I spend in this chair ever since getting hooked up to the Web. And *looking* like I'm working doesn't actually get the work done—nor even fool the boss, since I don't have a boss.

Still, as Paul Simon sings, these are the days of miracles and wonders. Thanks to the Internet, I can now finish work later than I used to and still make my deadlines, since an attached file gets to my editor a lot faster than real mail ever did.

The Unfinished Conversation

The old man died Sunday morning, finally releasing his tenacious hold on life. I had spoken to him a week earlier, shouting hello over the phone into his deaf ear across the distance of a thousand miles. I'm pretty sure he didn't know who I was. I'm positive he didn't understand me when I said I'd finally completed the book he'd been nagging me to finish, so he could read it.

When Grandpa Resnick died, I lost my biggest fan.

The book was the sequel to *In Legend Born*, a novel I dedicated to him. Grandpa read *In Legend Born* twice—all frigging 250,000 words of it—and immediately began nagging me to complete the next book. However, he fell seriously ill as I began writing the sequel, and by the time I finished it, he was so sick that he had given up reading my articles and short stories, never mind novels the size of compact cars.

Perhaps it's no coincidence that the heroine's elderly relative falls ill and dies in the book. Of course, this being an epic fantasy novel, the elderly character dies in active conflict with the forces of evil; not many characters in heroic fantasy get to die quietly in bed. But I knew the character *would* die. At some point early in the book, I understood that death was her destiny and that loss of a beloved elderly relative was part of the heroine's destiny.

No, it didn't have to be that way. I'm the writer, I can do anything I want. And I know some writers—including critically acclaimed writers—who don't like reading about the death of a young, or a beloved, or a likeable character, and who won't write such a death. Fair enough. A valid choice, I won't dispute it.

But that's them, and this is me. Ever since beloved pets and people first started dying on me, I've struggled with the universal experience of losing loved ones. And ever since I started writing, I've felt compelled to explore death and dying in my stories. Not as a morbid, bleak, existential obsession, but because I learned early on that when someone or something dies, life goes on for the rest of us, and it *should* go on; yet that's not always easy, nor does it always feel right. I struggle with this paradox as a person, and it captivates me as a writer. And—like most writers—I inevitably find myself writing about what captivates me.

It's fair to say that the death of my friend Fabian Cartwright in 1989 changed my life and my outlook—and therefore my work. He was a twenty-eight year old Irish actor whose career was starting to take off. I had abandoned my acting aspirations in favor of writing, and I'd abandoned Europe to return to the US, but we remained friends. During a hectic trip I made to London one summer, we kept trying to get together and kept failing. He overslept once, I couldn't show up once, he had to cancel once. Time ran out. Suddenly he was on his way to Barbados for an overdue vacation, and I was leaving England to meet a friend who had convinced me we should go to North

Africa in high summer (yes, in retrospect, my acquiescence con-founds me). Anyhow, in a few weeks, Fabian and I would both be back in London, and before he left again to start filming in Ireland and I left again to start writing a new book in America, we would finally sit down over dinner together for a few hours and catch up on everything. There was so much to talk about, and we made a fixed date which we agreed neither of us would miss for any reason.

A week later, a mutual friend sat me down to tell me he'd just received word that Fabian had died on vacation in Barbados. Fabian had seen someone drowning in the sea, had gone swim-ming out to help—and both of them drowned.

For months afterwards, I dreamed about him. He'd pop up, and we would have that long talk we'd been promising each other. I would deliberately not mention that he was dead, since I was afraid he'd have to leave if I reminded him. I suppose I only stopped dreaming about Fabian once I accepted that whether death comes slowly on lumbering wheels, with plenty of warning, or suddenly like an armed robber, you never do get to say everything you want to say. In the end, even if we'd had that dinner, our conversation would always be unfinished.

A year later, another friend of Fabian's and I both confessed to being furious at him. Who the hell did he think he was, swimming out into the sea to save a stranger from drowning? We doubted he was even that good a swimmer! How DARE he go and get himself killed with such a reckless decision?

Death is complicated. And living after someone else's death is *really* complicated.

Though I love a good sword-fighting film, I seldom watch Kenneth Brannagh's *Henry V*, because it's always such a strange shock to see Fabian (in a small role as one of the traitors whom

Henry orders executed early on), dead for many years now, still alive and talking (and talking, moreover, in a polished English manner very unlike his own Belfast accent). Maybe that uneasiness I feel whenever I see him onscreen is what led me to the idea of an entire cult in my fantasy novels that enables ordinary people to talk to their dead loved ones—and a hero who doesn't like to do it. Who knows? Maybe my guilt about not having phoned my Grandma Cain much in the final year of her life, when the dementia had swallowed up her mind, also led me to write about a dead relative whom this hero is forced to talk to while still consumed by guilt about his behavior toward that relative.

No, that book is not remotely autobiographical. For one thing, I didn't murder my grandma; and for another, I'm not destined to save the world. None of my fiction is autobiographical. But where do the roots of our work first germinate, if not in the things which have captivated our waking hours and haunted our sleeping ones?

When Fabian died, he was young, entering an exciting phase in his career, full of plans, meaning to meet me for dinner in a few weeks…He was *in the middle* of so much. In the middle of *life*.

When Fabian died, I learned that anyone can die anywhere at any time. Yes, I had known that intellectually. But after Fabian died, I understood it emotionally, and that changed me.

Perhaps that's why I then wrote a Silhouette, *The Bandit King*, wherein the entire storyline revolves around the unfinished business and ongoing secrets of someone who died young, in the middle of plans, in the middle of life. I also started writing science fiction/fantasy around that time, a genre well suited to exploring themes of death, loss, and sacrifice. Although I wrote a lot of humor, I also explored the sense of life's rightful pattern disrupted—and of this disruption *as* life's rightful pattern—as I tried to incorporate Fabian's death into the fabric of my life.

Because what I ultimately believe is that we must incorporate death into life, or we become bitter, cowardly, and squirrelly. Nonetheless, it's very hard, and it doesn't necessarily feel right. So I keep looking at this paradox as a writer. Young death, old death, real death, fake death, heroic and self-sacrificing death, tragic and unfair death, funny and unregretted death, painful and heartbreaking death. I go there over and over as a writer, because I go there over and over as a person. I've been making this trip since the first time a dog I loved died, and I'll keep going there until it's my turn to shuffle off this mortal coil.

My very first book, *One Sultry Summer*, a Silhouette Desire written when I was twenty-four and (frankly) fumbling with the craft, is about a couple who come together upon the death of a towering figure in both their lives. No, it's not (I repeat) autobiographical. But my Grandma Resnick had died a few years earlier, far away and with no funeral, and I think it was a natural impulse for me to explore, in my first real effort at writing, what we do after someone dies and is no longer there for us to thank or to castigate. I think it was inevitable that, even in my first Silhouette, I was drawn to the unfinished conversation.

I doubt there was even a connection in my mind between my life and the fictional lives in the book, but it did establish a pattern that has characterized my writing ever since—I'm a life thief. I suspect that most writers are, because you can only get so many ideas from late-night movies, cereal boxes, and newspaper stories. If you write about people and human relationships, sooner or later, your own life creeps into the shadows of your prose. Not in the "thinly disguised" manner of an aspiring literary writer who is convinced that his ordinary life will justify his tedious self-absorption by evolving into a bestselling novel of staggering genius; but in the manner of someone whose body of work reflects where she has been, what she has seen, and whom she's known.

By coincidence, just a few weeks before Grandpa Resnick died, I was proofreading a reprint edition of another book I'd dedicated to him, *Untouched By Man*. The heroine's grandfather, a rapscallion multi-millionaire whom no one in the family can control, is nothing like my intellectual and budget-conscious grandfather; and yet he is *very* like him in the lust for life and the sense of adventure he retains well into his eighth decade of life. My grandfather didn't go skydiving or catch strange diseases in the Amazon jungle as did my fictional character; but he did go on safari to Africa (twice), tour the Greek isles, and see the pyramids in his late seventies. In his early eighties, he still attended the World Science Fiction Convention regularly. When he was eighty-three, we took a trans-continental road-trip together when he decided to move from California to Florida. I still remember his scandalized complaints about all the dry counties we drove through in West Texas—Grandpa's overriding philosophy of life was that whatever you were doing, you should stop every ninety minutes to have a margarita.

My grandfather was almost certainly on a government list somewhere. Although he always preferred to talk about the present and the future, once in a while I got him to chat about the past—which is how I found out he was a Communist in his youth, and that he and my grandmother used to hang out at gay bars when they were dating, because that's where they found the most interesting conversations. He told me he became an ardent

Zionist during WWII when his best friend learned about the
death camps in Hitler's Europe; and he broke with the Zionist
movement after the newly-born Israeli government allowed
religious factions to have so much influence—because Grandpa
was also an ardent atheist.

He met my grandmother one day when they were in the
same crowded car, on their way to the beach with a group of
mutual friends. Only one person in the car besides Grandpa
knew all the verses to some slightly risqué song, and he decided
he had to get to know this girl better. By the end of the day,
they agreed to get married—so I never find novels about
whirlwind courtship hard to believe in. When I was a teenager,
Grandma told me my grandfather was her best friend and her
lover. (Of course, being a teen, I was totally grossed out by this
at the time; but now I appreciate it.) After forty years of marriage and ten years of widowhood, I once overheard Grandpa
describe Grandma to a friend of mine as "the love of my life."
So I don't think the happy endings of romance novels strain
credulity, either.

I have a picture of my grandmother in her bridal gown on
her wedding day. Her veil is askew because Grandpa's best friend
was weeping so copiously that he kept dropping the canopy
on her head during the ceremony. Aspects of the wedding were
rather hastily organized, since my grandfather (perhaps due to
the burden of being the only son in a Jewish household) couldn't
quite bring himself to explain to his mother that he was getting
married and leaving home. According to my grandmother, he
was cutting it awfully close by the time he finally broke the news
to his eccentric and impractical family. Needless to say, farce
seems a pretty reasonable form of fiction to me, and I've written

my fair share of it—including some with, go figure, eccentric and impractical families.

In his sixties, Grandpa even became a writer for a few years, which makes me the third generation in my family to pursue this vocation. He loved recounting the time he and my grandmother co-wrote a book about Teddy Kennedy and Chappaquiddick in just eight days, so it could be on the stands a mere two weeks after the incident occurred. (No, he did not write this—or anything else—under his real name.)

The old man died Sunday morning, and life goes on without him, as it should. Our conversation is unfinished, and it always will be. There were more things I meant to ask, more things I meant to say. There will be more of my work that I want to give him to read. There will be more books by other people that I want to send him, because he was a voracious reader who enjoyed chatting with me about books I'd recommended to him. There will be more bars I'll know he'd have liked. More bands he'd have enjoyed hearing. (Grandma was always one to say, as everyone else started fading around 1:00 AM, "Let's stay for another set!") More arguments we'd have had wherein he'd have shouted, "You're an idiot," which was his way of expressing friendly disagreement.

What I've learned over the years is that when the person ends, the relationship doesn't. Grandpa will never do anything new hereafter, but he lives on in my memory. The conversation continues, forever unfinished, though it does become a little one-sided. And, at least in this instance, I know exactly what the old man would say if he were here right now:

"Have a margarita, kid."

The Long Haul

One day a concom (committee in charge of a science fiction/fantasy convention) convinces me to drive a truck, loaded with supplies for the con, from its storage warehouse in one city to the con site in another city. The vehicle is roughly the size of a small U-Haul truck, the kind recommended for hauling the household goods of a studio apartment. I'm a little nervous, since I usually drive a compact car. However, I have driven a truck this size before, so I agree to haul the load.

Once I find myself on the road, though, things start to go haywire. I thought there'd be a navigator or co-driver; but, no, I am completely alone for the whole ride. I thought I would drive the truck about 100 miles; but, no, the distance keeps increasing—300 miles, 500 miles, 800, 950, 1,200... No end in sight. My destination keeps stretching into the distance, always farther and farther away.

Darkness falls, and dawn never comes. The night seems eternal. I'm worried. I've never driven a vehicle this size in the dark before. And speaking of size...The truck is getting bigger.

Much, *much* BIGGER. It grows to the size of a four-bedroom household moving-van by the time I reach the state line. Before long, it's a massive eighteen-wheeler. The cab alone is bigger than my first apartment, and the load has become so huge that, looking in my side mirrors, I can't tell where the rear of the truck ends. Such a big load is incredibly unwieldy, very hard to steer or maneuver. It also picks up speed with alarming ease.

I now realize it's not only pitch dark outside, but also snowing. Visibility is poor, the road is slick, and traction unpredictable. I need to slow down...but the brakes are sluggish, and the sheer momentum of this vast, dense leviathan ensures that I keep plunging ahead into the night.

Next thing I know, I'm suddenly on a city street instead of the interstate, and I'm side-swiping hundreds of parallel-parked cars. My massive eighteen-wheeler careens wildly around the road, destroying vehicles and wiping out parking meters, lamp posts, and (as I enter a gas station) gas pumps—some of which fly dramatically into the air, followed by geysers of gasoline.

Happily, this slows down the truck enough that I am finally able to bring it to a halt. Shaking and sweating with terror, I climb out of the cab and go sit on a street curb, where I stare wearily at the wreckage this endeavor has wrought.

I look at the truck. It's even *bigger* now. (Is there such a thing as a twenty-six-wheeler?). I realize it's just too big, too massive, too hard to control, and the distance is far too great. I can't get this load to the con. I know the concom needs the goods I'm hauling, and I swore I'd deliver; but I can't get back in the cab of that truck. I just *can't*.

Now someone from the concom happens along. He surveys the wreckage of the gas station, the neighborhood, and my own shattered self. Then he hands me a cup of coffee.

"Come on, Resnick," he says. "It has to be done, and there's no one but you to finish the job. Get back in the damn truck and deliver the goods already."

I sigh in resignation, get back in the truck, and turn on the engine. I check the side mirrors, looking behind me; I see nothing but the load I'm hauling, extending so high and wide and far back that nothing else in the whole world is visible. I look ahead at the dark, icy, endless road before me...and I pull the truck out of the ruined gas station. Because I have to deliver the goods. Because it's my job. Because there's no one else who can finish this journey for me...

And I wake up in a cold sweat, heart pounding with terror and dread.

Gosh, guess it's time to start another day's work.

Welcome to my world. The daily life of an epic fantasy novelist.

❉

I sit staring blankly at the cursor on the computer screen. I look at the current page number of my very-late and still-unfinished novel. This book is already longer than my first six books put together—and it's still not done.

There is reputedly a higher rate of manic-depressive illness among poets than among novelists, and a higher rate of such disorders among novelists than among mundanes. No one has ever studied the rate of mental illness among epic writers as compared to other novelists, but I'll bet the numbers go through the roof.

Mwha-ha-ha-ha-ha-ha-ha! [Sob!]

❉

I started my career by writing short series-romance novels for Silhouette, an imprint of Harlequin Enterprises (otherwise known to romance writers as the Evil Empire). I wasn't suited to series-romance, but I liked writing short books. Hell, I like *reading* short books. The biggest irony of my career may be that you have to tie me to a chair at gunpoint to make me read a book as long as some of the fantasy novels I write.

Anyhow, after a dozen books for Silhouette, I wrote my first "big" romance, *Fever Dreams*, and I discovered that 100,000 words was not a difficult length, after all, despite my initial fears. I felt I could write that length regularly without struggling. Cool!

Then [*sinister music*] I pitched a fantasy proposal to my agent. He liked it, but he advised me that if I could find a good way to turn that initial two-small-books idea into one big epic story, we could get a much better sale.

I resisted the suggestion. I explained about only reading short books. I explained about preferring to write short books. I'd recently seen a family photo of *New York Times* bestseller Tad Williams' adult cat, sitting upright, completely dwarfed by Tad's epic fantasy manuscript sitting next to it. I explained emphatically to my agent that I would not do that. I would *never* do that. It was out of the question. No way.

I wound up doing it. And we got a good sale.

Now I continue to stare at the blinking cursor on page 1,416 of my current book. From where we start out, how do we ever reach where we wind up?

✳

The late James Clavell once said that the only way he could write books like *Shogun* and *Noble House* was by always

believing, at the start of a novel that *this* time things would be
different. *This* time, that wouldn't happen to him.

How did a manuscript the size of a small horse simply
"happen" to someone, I wondered?

Now I know. Like the road to hell, you make the journey
moment by moment, unable to see through the dark and the
snow...until you one day realize that your truck is bigger than
Cleveland, and it's too late to turn back.

At page 100 of this book, I had not yet introduced all of
my plotlines or main characters. I had a *crise des nerfs* around
page 500. I recalled that when my editor read my last book,
which was 978 pages when I turned it in, his revision letter
ensured that I added about twenty-five pages to the final version. Now, at page 500, I could already tell that I would have a
nervous breakdown if I heard those words again: "It's so tight,
it could be even longer."

At page 800, I started to get morose. Around page 950,
I fell into a deep depression, living only on Oreo cookies
and refusing to answer the phone. I realized I had made a
disastrous miscalculation. Being relatively new to epic fiction,
I began this book (a sequel) fearing that I didn't have enough
conflict to carry another 250,000-word story; so I developed
lots of new conflict to accompany the conflict left over from
the prequel, thus ensuring this book wouldn't be a heavily-pad-
ded bore.

Works in theory.

In practice, I now perceived that the story had become
so complex that there was no possible way I could wrap it up
in a mere 250,000 words. It was also too late to remove a few
plotlines and keep the book "short." I'd created a fabric of
multiple storylines that all gradually weave together toward

a series of interrelated climaxes. Pull out one thread, and the whole tapestry would unravel.

I'd originally thought this was good structure. Now I saw that it had put me in the cab of a twenty-six-wheeler leviathan on a dark, icy road with no way out, and no one else to complete the journey for me.

Around page 1,200, I realized that I couldn't finish this book around page 1,200. (*Nothing* slips past me!) Realizing that I was already over my contracted story-length, I confessed to my agent, who confessed to my editor. To paraphrase their responses: "Come on, Resnick. It has to be done, and there's no one but you to finish the job. Get back in the damn truck and deliver the goods already."

I proceeded to page 1,201. To page 1,416. To page 1,732, where I finally, weeping with relief, wrote the words "The End."

Because it's my job. Because I swore I'd deliver the goods. Because no one else can make this journey for me.

❋

The long-dark-haul of epic fantasy is the private little hell in which I was destined to burn. Your private hell may be different; and I don't want to burn there any more than you want to burn in mine. *Vive la différence!* Whether I chose this load or it somehow chose me, I'm still at the wheel and going straight on 'til dawn.

That book, all 1,732 pages of it, is my message from hell (where a beachside cabana is cheaper than you'd think), delivered in a bottle the size of a Mack truck, written on a stack of paper that makes whole forests fear my name: In the end, a writer's work must always be its own reward, because that's all you can count on when you're careening down that dark, icy highway, all alone for the long haul—be it 2,000 words or 1,732 pages. This is the gospel according to a mad epicist.

Meanwhile, if you're wondering how they published a book that big, the answer is: They didn't. Fourteen months after delivery, my publisher suddenly noticed it was 1,732 pages—*nothing* slips past them!—and declared with gasps of surprise that they couldn't publish it at that length. So it came out as two books, *The White Dragon* and *The Destroyer Goddess*.

OW! OW! OWWWW!!!

"A critic," a friend recently quoted to me, "is someone who goes out on the field after the battle and shoots the wounded."

One of the most professionally educational books I've ever read is *No Turn Unstoned*, compiled by actress Diana Rigg. The book is a collection of some of the most devastating and venomous theatrical reviews ever written. *No Turn Unstoned* taught me several valuable lessons about reviews before I ever began my writing career. It thereby helped me gain a sense of perspective that I desperately need on occasions when I read comments about my work like this one (from an Amazon.com reader review): "The one good recommendation I can give [the book] is that it is a great cure for insomnia."

One of the things I learned when I read *No Turn Unstoned* is that there have been nasty critics almost as long as there have been writers and actors. Rigg's book quotes scathing theatrical reviews written by social commentators as early as the sixth century B.C. Another useful lesson I keep in mind is that no writer or actor has ever completely eluded the venom of a critic's pen. Dorothy Parker wrote of Katharine Hepburn's performance in a 1933 play, *The Lake*, that she ran the gamut of emotion from A to B. When Oscar Wilde's *The Importance of Being Ernest* first opened, a reviewer wrote, "The thing seemed to me so helpless, so crude, so bad, clumsy, feeble, and vulgar..." Bertrand Russell said of George Bernard Shaw's *Man and Superman*, "It disgusted me." Imagine, for a moment, being the actress of whom a critic wrote, "What a personality that girl needs." Diana Rigg, still my heroine from her days as the elegant and deadly Mrs. Peel in *The Avengers*, bravely includes a casually vicious review about herself, from *New York Magazine*, which she found so wounding that, "I remember making my way to the theatre the following day, darting from doorway to doorway and praying I wouldn't meet anyone I knew."

And speaking of casually vicious reviews...

"Soapy and predictable and long-winded" is what *Kirkus* said about a novel of mine. *Kirkus* also said of a romantic suspense novel by Carole Bellacera, "It's neither romantic nor suspenseful." Indeed, *Kirkus* reviews are so notoriously nasty that I've heard the publicity department at my publishing house makes a game of deliberately culling any accidentally positive phrases from bad *Kirkus* reviews and using them for promotional purposes. If true, this would explain why they went to all the trouble of culling a comically brief quote ("Well handled") from the scathing *Kirkus* review of *In Legend Born*, even though there were enough good reviews of the book that this certainly wasn't necessary. (The *Kirkus* review from which they culled this two-word "praise" indicated that a couple of minor elements are well handled in an otherwise awful novel.)

Now that I think of it, though—what a great game! I can

hardly wait for *Kirkus'* blistering review of my next novel so that I can play, too!

However, I am forced to admit that *Kirkus'* scathing review of my book is a fair and valid example of a bad review; it simply expresses a negative opinion of the work. No matter how painful the writer may find such commentary, this is a legitimate (even necessary) function of a book reviewer.

As reviewer, editor, and author Ann Lafarge notes, the issues a reviewer should address in a review are: "Did the writer accomplish what he was trying to do? If so, how? If not, why not?" Novelist P.G. Nagle suggests, "Negative reviews should be stated in a rational manner. Any person with a reasonable command of both himself and the English language should be able to express a negative opinion without resorting to insult. Objections should be explained, and opinionated statements should be supported."

Art is subjective; therefore, of course, opinions about a novel will always be varied, and often even conflicting. I certainly don't *enjoy* bad reviews, but I accept that disliking my work is a perfectly fair and valid response when reviewing it.

However, when reviewers get absorbed in their own speculative theories, make inaccurate accusations, are deliberately cruel, or get inappropriately personal, many writers—understandably—get annoyed.

Bill Peschel, a reviewer for a newspaper in South Carolina, once wrote that mystery author Tamar Myers was obviously "trying to write like Carolyn Hart and Joan Hess, but fails miserably," and added that "the book smells of flopsweat." Since Myers had never read Hart or Hess at that point in her career, the real mystery is how she could possibly have been trying to emulate them. "And," Myers wonders, "what the hell is flopsweat? Sixteen very successful books later I would like to present Mr. Peschel with a vial of vile flopsweat."

A critic in Albany said in a review of Tess Gerritsen's *Gravity*: "She has seen her books reach the best-seller lists, but it's almost impossible to understand why." In a review of *Bloodstream*, this same critic wrote, "[Gerritsen's] success as a writer is a sorry indicator of how far the book-buying public's standards have sunk. If quality was the determining factor, Gerritsen [a doctor] might well be on the phone as we speak, contacting health care companies for per-diem work." Perhaps you've already noticed that in two sentences comprising a total of more than forty words, this reviewer hasn't actually said a single thing about *Bloodstream* itself, but has instead spent his time castigating Gerritsen's readers and attempting to humiliate Gerritsen. Moreover, this reviewer was evidently too busy being clever to bother actually *reading*, since both of these reviews were based on audio books. I agree with Gerritsen, who asks, "How can reviewers judge our books based on an audio [version] that includes only about a third of our text?"

The reviewer in Albany isn't alone in writing vicious reviews of Gerritsen's work. A *Publisher's Weekly* review of her suspense novel *Harvest* said snidely: "Will surprise only readers who move their lips." Happily for Gerritsen, *Harvest* went on to become her first hardcover *New York Times* bestseller.

And speaking of snide *Publishers Weekly* reviews...

Mystery series author Kathy Lynn Emerson endured this gem in *Publishers Weekly*: "Forecast: The thinness of the last two or three books of what started as a solid historical series suggests the author has lost interest and is just churning them out; readers will continue to lose interest as well." Personally, I'm quite taken with the delusions of omniscience revealed here. Despite the evidence we've just seen, with regard to *Harvest*, that *PW* reviewers' tastes are clearly not in lock-step with readers' tastes, this *PW* reviewer now goes well past stating his own response to the current book and chooses to predict how readers will respond to Emerson's future work. Moreover, the reviewer presumes to know what's in the writer's mind, claiming (erroneously) that Emerson has grown bored with her own work. Finally, he also deliberately insults the writer with the (also erroneous) phrase "churning them out." Really, it boggles my mind to see this reviewer taking so many missteps in a single sentence.

Years ago, historian Barbara Tuchman took *PW* to task when one of their anonymous reviewers claimed that Tuchman's latest book contained historical inaccuracies. By the time Tuchman was done with *PW*, it was clear that the reviewer had merely used the shield of anonymity to make unfounded accusations which he couldn't prove or defend. Ever since then, I've wondered why anyone thinks there's anything of value in *anonymous* reviews in any forum.

Frankly, I despise anyone who exercises the privilege of publicly criticizing a writer's work but who is unwilling to *identify himself* in his public comments. I consider such behavior beneath contempt.

I also think that anonymous reviews are pointless, in that they inherently suggest that all people are alike and will all respond the same way to a book. How absurd! After all, one editor considers a given novel unpublishable while another loves it and snaps it up. I have friends whose reading recommendations I take, and friends whose tastes I've learned are so different from mine that I deliberately avoid their recommendations. So if I don't know the identity of the reviewer and can't learn his tastes, of what possible use is a review to me as a reader or a movie-goer? Publishing anonymous reviews, in addition to being morally contemptible, suggests that I'm such a dolt that I'm willing to be guided by *anyone's* opinion, without having the slightest idea upon what tastes it's based.

And speaking of anonymous reviews…

One of the biggest changes we've seen in the world of book reviewing in recent years is the Internet making available an ever-expanding number of opportunities for readers to review books in public forums. The Internet has reader e-lists, reader bulletin boards, reader online fanzines, small start-up online magazines that publish reviews provided by readers, and online bookstores that encourage readers to post reviews of the books they read.

While this has been great for readers in numerous ways, it can be a mixed blessing for novelists. I myself very rarely read my reviews on Amazon.com, the online bookseller best known for its reader reviews. *New York Times* bestseller Teresa Medeiros perfectly sums up my feelings about it: "I'm embarrassed to admit that I'm a complete wimp when it comes to Amazon reader reviews. They cut me to the heart. They leave a lingering ache in my stomach. They suck the creative soul right out of me…I enjoy the good reviews, but sometimes even those are disconcerting, like having somebody watch you go to the bathroom. And it doesn't matter if a book has fifty positive reviews, it's that one negative one that will haunt me for days." Exactly!

Indeed, many writers struggle with the phenomenon of Amazon.com's reader reviews. What bothers writers about reader reviews are the same things that cause them to complain about professional reviews; writers wince when a review is deliberately vicious, but it makes them nuts when a reader, as Jean Ross Ewing a.k.a. Julia Ross puts it, makes accusations or statements that simply aren't true. As an example, Ewing cites an Amazon.com reader review of her award-winning novel *Flowers Under the Ice*, which this particular reader review describes as "creepy." The reviewer claims the book's love story is "sadistic," and she clearly implies the hero is sexually abusive, even a rapist. Ewing says, "I believe it unfairly misrepresents the book, as well as making horrendous implications about my sexual philosophy." (Having read the book myself, by the way, I find the reader's comments perplexing.)

Moving from the surreal to the absurd…A bad Amazon.com reader review for Patricia Bray's *The Irish Earl* complains the book was a disappointment because (wait for it!), "One literally had to read the entire book until the conflict was resolved." (Damn! All these years in the business, and I never knew I was supposed to wrap up the conflict halfway through the book!) An Amazon.com reader review slammed *Mr. Perfect* because, the book's bestselling author Linda Howard says, "I didn't write at least one paragraph about the heroine emptying the cat's litter box. Obviously litter plays a big part in this woman's life, and she was outraged that I didn't acknowledge it." Novelist Ann Chamberlin received a furious review from a reader who apparently doesn't know what a fantasy novel is, and who doesn't necessarily seem to know what *fiction* is. Speaking of fantasy, an Amazon reader says that I seem "to falter in the historical department somewhat;" the work in question is a fantasy novel set in a make-believe world that I invented, so I have no idea what "historical" flaws the reader could be talking about.

Accusing the author of bad research or historical inaccuracy is, by the way, a common habit of professional and amateur reviewers which many writers find particularly aggravating; especially since such critics very rarely present credentials for their "superior" knowledge of the author's subject matter, let alone make specific citations of the inaccuracies they claim to have found. A bookseller who writes reviews for the *Denver Post* reveals a strange reason for reading historical mysteries when he writes of three books he's reviewing (two of which are by acquaintances of mine): "All three provide just enough historical inaccuracies to make knowledgeable readers feel sufficiently superior to the authors…" Clearly self-deluding reviewers will also feel superior.

Another common habit of critics which makes writers grind their teeth is that of claiming the author is unsuccessfully attempting to copy a given novel or novelist. One newspaper reviewer, for example, accused Linda Howard of stealing the plot of Oscar Wilde's *Portrait of Dorian Gray*, a novel she had never read and which she later learned, in fact, bore no resemblance whatsoever to her own. (Having read both books, I can testify that the reviewer's accusation is indeed inexplicable.)

Overall, the conclusion I've come to over the years is that nasty and sloppy book reviewers would probably go about their work very differently if *they* were victims of the sort of careless, ignorant, and scathing public commentary that we must regularly endure as novelists. Since that's not likely to happen soon, however, I continue to follow advice that an acting teacher of mine, years ago, attributed to Sir Lawrence Olivier: "If the reviews are bad, you can't believe them. If the reviews are good, you can't believe them. Your job is just to go out there and do your very best work every show, eight shows per week."

Sure, it's hard to face the blank page after reading a bad review; but at least it's not as hard as facing a *live audience* right after I read a comment like, "Resnick's attempt to make you like the characters failed miserably. Altogether a boring and unenjoyable book."

I'll Just Sit Here In The Dark

I'm at the opera tonight.

Some of you, I feel sure, are already groaning. The *opera*? Egad! Even the wailing of off-key bagpipes is not such tooth-cracking torture as the climactic notes of a coloratura soprano at the end of a long aria about (inevitably) her emotional misery, or her unrequited love, or her approaching death due to a terminal disease which is mysteriously unable to impair her ability to deliver high notes loud enough to be heard six counties away.

Plus, opera is performed in other languages, making it impossible for us to follow what's going on. Not that that really matters, since relatively little of importance is ever said sung. The lead tenor can babble musically for twenty minutes without moving the plot forward one little step! And when a translation is provided (on a tiny screen which you need bin-oculars to read), it usually reads something like: "Let me die. Let me die. Let me die." If I wrote dialogue that dull, I'd be out of work before the singer had time to draw breath for the next line (which probably reads: "I'm so unhappy. I'm so unhappy. I'm so unhappy.").

This, I sense, is what you're thinking.

At any rate, it's certainly what I was thinking the first time I ever attended the opera—which was when my mother asked me to go to a production of Don Giovanni with her because my father insisted that thirty-five years of marriage did not entitle her to force him to sit through three hours of opera. I figured that keeping my mother company at Don Giovanni was probably an easy way of perceiving myself as a good daughter (a perception which I rarely pursue in any proactive way), so I agreed to go.

I brought a book with me, just in case.

As it happens, I never opened that book. From the moment the performance began, I was riveted. I was a convert. I became, if not an opera fanatic, then at least someone who really likes some works of opera.

Don Giovanni is, after all, that pinnacle of my own art: a good story well told. The music is engaging, the characters are compelling, the lyrics are witty, the plot twists work well, and the conclusion is satisfying. This was not (as you may have gathered) what I had expected. Delighted to have been so wrong, I have been attending operas ever since.

And thank goodness, too! Last year, I sold a fantasy novel which first occurred to me while attending Puccini's Turandot. I was captivated by the shiny exoticism and dark corruption of the kingdom portrayed in this opera. I was entranced by the lush eroticism woven into the physical danger and the moral decay that permeate this crumbling monarchy. I sat there in the dark with only part of my attention on Puccini's soaring music; the rest of my mind was absorbed with what kind of story I would write in such a setting. That very night, I started making notes for a tale which I'd never have thought of—let alone sold—if I had not seen Turandot.

Tonight's opera, however, is not proving so inspiring to me. Elektra, by Richard Strauss, is dissonant, bleak, and depressing. But then, what did I expect of a German composer's rendition of a Greek tragedy? (The tickets were complimentary.)

Electra's mother conspired with her paramour to kill Electra's father, Agamemnon, and Electra is taking it badly, go figure. The opera opens with everyone singing about how crazy Electra seems lately. Then a crazy woman emerges from beneath the floorboards and, sure enough, she's Electra. She spends a while in high-pitched wailing about her emotional misery (okay, so there's a reason we have this image of opera). Electra craves vengeance for her father's murder—a man about whom she expresses such strong feelings that, well, it's pretty obvious someone should have found this girl a boyfriend years ago.

However, when we finally meet Clytemnestra, Electra's murderous mother, it's really easy to see how Electra grew up to be such a basket case. It's initially a little harder to figure out how an over-dressed, shrill virago like Clytemnestra got herself a handsome lover like Aegisthus; but then one realizes that an ambitious man might have looked past the queen's unpleasant personality to perceive the long-term advantages of assisting in her quest for sexual satisfaction and early widowhood. That is to say, Aegisthus has what we in the trade call motivation.

Perhaps my experiences as an opera-goer are an example of how some operas (such as the exotic and sinister grandeur of Turandot) are inspiration for epic fantasy writers, while other operas (the psychotically dysfunctional family life of Elektra, for example) are evidently inspiration for modern literary writers. I'm already so depressed that I'd like to kill Clytemnestra myself so we could all go home now. However, I'm in the balcony and can't get to the stage. So I sit here in the dark and listen to her and Electra bitch at each other in a minor key.

And, boy, can Clytemnestra bitch. I squint and read the translation of the German lyrics as Clytemnestra sings that she's so fed up with her crazy daughter that "my eyelids swell and my liver is sick."

I decide to stop reading the translations until we get through this all-too-biological portion of the opera. I just sit here in the dark and listen to the talented cast singing in a language that I, thank goodness, don't understand.

Sitting here in the dark is something I've been doing all my life, in fact. I don't know when my parents first took me to a play, but You're a Good Man Charlie Brown is the first one I remember. When Snoopy sang like the rest of the cast, I wasn't surprised. I'd known all along that dogs were that smart.

At the age of seven, although sick with a bad cold, I refused to miss the Broadway touring company's performance of 1776 in my native Chicago. I was young enough to be confused about the characters' genders because they all had long hair and frilly clothes, so I freely pictured myself in many of the roles—particularly that of the young soldier who sings a heart-rending ballad about dying on the battlefield while his mother looks for his body. The plaintive sorrow in his voice, the wrenching lyrics, and those captivating moments as I sat in the dark have stayed with me for over thirty years.

Most of all, though, I remember the gripping tension I felt as the Second Continental Congress furiously debated the question of American independence. As June turned to July onstage, Adams, Jefferson, and Franklin faced overwhelming odds in their struggle for a seemingly impossible dream. I wanted to weep with anxiety as I rooted for the Congress to sign Jefferson's document and bring forth a new nation—the very nation where I was born free almost two hundred years after this play takes place. I knew how the story ended, but I was nonetheless on the edge of my seat until the actors finally ratified the Declaration of Independence as the pages of their onstage calendar turned to July 4, 1776.

Now that's good storytelling.

It's not what the reader already knows, it's what you make her believe in and care about while she's reading. I learned this while sitting in the dark.

Now, sitting in the dark again so many years later, I risk opening my eyes to see where we're at in this story.

Clytemnestra, still in a pissy mood, is complaining about people "exposing their abscesses and boils to the breeze."

I hastily close my eyes and continue my reflections.

My favorite musical is Man of La Mancha. Probably because it's about a writer. (I am as transparent as glass, as constant as the sun, as self-absorbed as the next guy.)

The Man in question is the sixteenth century Spanish author Miguel de Cervantes, who was imprisoned at Argamasilla in La Mancha due to some financial irregularities (and what writer can't identify with that?). Stuck in a cell with criminals and vagabonds in the first scene of Man of La Mancha, Cervantes invites them into the world of his imagination—into the tale of Don Quixote, the knight of the woeful countenance who tilts at windmills believing they're giants, and who perceives a bitter tavern wench as the noble lady whom he loves, Dulcinea. Just as Don Quixote changes the world he sees with his impossible dreams, so does Cervantes change the world of the prison with his writer's imagination, with the gifts of the storyteller, with the visionary conviction of the novelist.

We are the magicians of the mind, and I learned this while sitting in the dark.

I hear a new voice on the stage now and open my eyes again. Orestes, who is Electra's brother, has finally arrived on the scene. He seems understandably shocked to discover how badly things have gone at home during his absence. He's been gone so long that his sister doesn't even recognize him. And I know just enough Greek mythology to realize that he should never have come back. As a result of what happens next, Orestes will be pursued by the Furies—who make his mother Clytemnestra seem like pleasant company.

Now he starts singing about abscesses. It's clearly a family obsession.

I go back to drifting.

I live in Cincinnati, a conservative city famous for ignoring the First Amendment. Thus, it was that a controversial, low-budget Canadian play, Poor Superman, decided to make its U.S. debut here a few years ago. The producers were reputedly counting on the predictable local uproar (and the probable attempts to ban the play here) to provide enough free publicity to get national attention for the play. Naturally, I went to see it.

Poor Superman is about a married man who, much to his own surprise, enters into a passionate love affair—with another man. The experimental theatre which hosted the play here is a small place, and we happened to wind up sitting in the front row. Practically on the stage. The actors were often within a few feet of us. So, during the big love scene, when the two male leads start passionately stroking and kissing each other's stark naked bodies…and doing this so close to me that I could have touched them both with only a little effort…I sat there in mute panic, thinking, "Please don't either of you fellows get an erection. Just don't. Should I look away? Should I close my eyes? Should I just keep watching as if I'm not obsessing about your genitals? Aren't you done kissing and touching yet? Because if this goes on any longer, one of you could have an involuntary reaction, if you get my drift! And I am a total stranger sitting within four damn feet of you, in case you hadn't NOTICED!"

Though my seat wasn't as dark as usual, the writing lesson was very memorable: Don't ever pull your reader out of the frame.

Bad research. Anachronistic writing. Self-serving polemics and lectures barely disguised as narrative. Incongruity and lack of continuity. Weak characterization, leaden pacing, lack of motivation, stiff dialogue, lazy plotting…There are a thousand ways for a novelist to wind up naked onstage while an appalled audience obsesses about her exposed genitals at a critical moment. So to speak.

As soon as I am reminded that the characters are only figments, the story loses me. I stop thinking about them and their story; I become riveted on my story again—in this case, my own anxiety about an embarrassing moment in a public place.

Our real flesh-and-blood existence dominates our senses and our thoughts so insistently that fiction can only prevail by being even more powerful than life. More vivid, more colorful, more intense, more compelling. Every page we write has to be so good that it eclipses the reader's reality while she's reading it. If we can't do that, then we can't hold our audience.

I learned this by sitting in the dark.

After worrying about abscesses and condemning the sins of the flesh, Electra and Orestes finally enact their plan.

They assassinate Clytemnestra and her ambitious paramour, Aegisthus. There's also a bloody body that's been lying around on stage for a while. Since my eyes were closed for so long, I don't know whose it is. But based on the way Electra fondles it, I suspect it's the over-ripe corpse of her father, Agamemnon. (This girl needs help.)

Next, Electra keels over dead, worn out from all the grief and vengeance and sustained high notes.

Hooray! The end! We can finally go home!

If the audience is eager to leave the theatre, it occurs to me, then the opera has failed. (At least with this audience member.)

The word opera literally means "work."

Our work as writers is to keep the reader lingering in the story, savoring its taste, satisfied with the ending yet sorry to have reached it. Our stories should live with the reader as welcome ghosts after the last page is turned. Our task is to keep the reader applauding even after the curtain has fallen and the house lights have come up. Our work is to bring the reader back, season after season, until, like Electra, our song wears us out and we sink into the ground, forever silent.

This is what I've learned, so far, from sitting here in the dark.

Labelismization

My friend Karen travels a lot on business. She says business travel used to be a lot more interesting, because different towns and cities had different shops and restaurants. She enjoyed the unfamiliar, relished experimenting with the unknown, and had fun discovering unique local businesses wherever she went.

All of that, Karen says mournfully, has changed. It seems to her that wherever she goes these days, she sees exactly the same restaurants and exactly the same stores—all the national chains that have spread across the face of our nation like wildfire in recent years. You can go to fifty cities in America and eat exactly the same meal in exactly the same restaurant in every city. You can buy the same pair of pants at exactly the same store in every city. Life in America, Karen tells me, is becoming generic.

Then why can't I get a really good corned beef sandwich anywhere except Chicago, I ask? Karen ignores me and continues with her thesis that includes one complaint which I hear a lot from readers: Too many novels that are being released are exactly like too many other novels that are being released.

This is, of course, a familiar problem to working novelists, many of whom feel that individualistic work is often neglected and ignored by the publishing industry, if it's even published at all. It's common knowledge among us that in order to be saleable, a novel has to be marketable; and in order to be marketable, it has to fit a publisher's extant notions of what they can market. I don't know about you, but I've received more than one rejection letter over the years saying, in effect, "This work is good, but we don't know how to market it, so we're not buying it."

My friend Julie (who grew up with me and Karen) is vice president of an advertising firm, and she is always aghast when I tell her that marketing people in publishing rarely seem to deal with (or, at least, invest effort in) a product they don't *already* know how to market. But the purpose of a marketing department, Julie tells me, is to figure out how to sell the product, not to limit the company to producing what the marketing department already knows how to sell.

Let's review: The purpose of a marketing department is to figure out how to sell the product.

Wow! Is that a neat concept, or *what*? Why did no one tell us about this before now?

However, in fairness to publishers (yes, even I can be fair on occasion), I must acknowledge that they do sometimes try something new. Remember when Harper and Bantam first experimented with replacing the romance genre's traditional clinch covers with something readers *wouldn't* be embarrassed to be seen reading? Wasn't that cool? Remember when Delacorte decided to get behind a first-person point-of-view, gazillion-word romance novel, *Outlander*, which they gave away at the Romance Writers of America annual national conference to help create word-of-mouth for it? Didn't it give you warm fuzzies that a publisher would do that for someone who wasn't a sex-addict-politician or a movie star?

Remember when Avon signed cover model Fabio to be a romance "novelist?" Well, okay, yes, some new ideas suck canal water.

Indeed, it's that whole nasty canal water possibility that accounts for something that writer and former marketing analyst Valerie Taylor once said to me, which is that publishers all want to be the *second* one to discover a new trend, a new subgenre, a new commercial wave; they want to be second, because being *first* involves risk, and publishers hate risk. (In other words, "If it's never been tried before...then, my *God*, man, let's not try it HERE!")

While I'm feeling fair, though, I should also quote Tom Doherty, CEO of Tor Books, who has said more than once that every book is a new-product launch; and, as anyone in business knows, new-product launches are always risky. If the last bottle of Ivory dishwashing liquid you bought satisfied you, it's almost certain that the next bottle of Ivory dishwashing liquid you buy will satisfy you, too. Whereas if the last Laura Resnick novel you bought satisfied you, it's still a complete toss-up whether or not you'll like the next one, or read three chapters and then give it to your dog as a chew toy.

This is one of the reasons that publishing is a business of many failures and narrow profit-margins. Of course, any reasonable writer can understand a publisher's desire to make profits and stay in business. Unfortunately, though, this too often translates into a publisher doing more of what has already been done-to-death, conveying an impression that publishers think books are like dishwashing liquid and that writers are mass-assembly workers.

As a natural consequence of this, writers (and also reviewers) often make unhappy (even sneering) comments about "brand-name authors." I must say, actually, I think most brand-name authors are remarkably polite about the way they're regularly eviscerated in the press (and even by other writers) as examples of America's descent into generic art forced on a helpless public by vast corporate entities.

In fact, brand-name writers are often highly original. In most cases, they invented the trends they created. Take a look at Crichton, Steel, King, and Grisham, to name just a few. There was relatively little like their books in the marketplace when they each came along; it's only in the wake of their enormous success that a truly astonishing proliferation of eerily similar books emerged, too often in a rampage that neglected quality and originality in favor of marketability ("A Novel In The Tradition Of..." yada yada yada). Because now that someone had demonstrated how to drive a specific type of novel to blockbuster success, many others jumped on the bandwagon, milked the cash cow, and thereby produced the sea of coattail-riding books of stultifying similarity that make brand-name writers seem generic.

This is the modern American way. This is the era of mass marketing, of a vast consumer economy driven by pursuing someone *else's* success. This pattern is the same from dinner appetizers, to movies, to tampons. The success of a thing compels mavens in virtually every industry to contemplate how to benefit from that new-product success with their own version of the exact same thing. Consequently, you could lose your mind trying to figure out which brand of breath-freshening-tartar-control toothpaste to buy, which TV show about a group of twenty-something friends to watch, and which movie about a disaster in outer-space to go see.

As each success is perceived more and more narrowly, whole new incredibly specific categories spring up overnight. And this trend grows and multiplies until, if you're like me, you're utterly bewildered by the categorization, sub-categorization, and sub-sub-categorization of fiction in the modern publishing industry in which you work.

For example, I have seen a novel of mine, *In Legend Born*, described as: epic fantasy; romantic fantasy; heroic fantasy; traditional fantasy; historical fantasy; high fantasy. It's just one book, and—though I daresay it's a good one—it is not all things to all readers. Nor did I *try* to write a book which could be described as six different kinds of fiction, though at least some of those descriptions are apt. (Just to clarify, *I* call it epic fantasy.)

The really confusing thing, though, is that these are all extant sub-categorizations of the fantasy market—and there are others, too. Moreover, that's just half the genre, the genre being science fiction/fantasy. So, along with fantasy, there's also science fiction and all of its fruitfully multiplying sub-categorizations, from hard science fiction, to cyberpunk, to literary science fiction, to space opera (which, like bodice rippers, no one admits to writing).

These days, you can't just write a mystery novel; you're supposed to know what *kind* of mystery novel you're writing: Cozy? Medical thriller? Police procedural? Legal thriller? You can't just tell your agent you're preparing a romance proposal, you've got to specify: Historical paranormal? Romantic suspense? Sweet contemporary? Traditional Regency? Is it a time-travel paranormal or a supernatural paranormal? Is it a Regency-era historical romance, or a Western historical romance? Or it is, oops!, a romantic historical mainstream?

This gets even more confusing for a writer who is versatile—not to mention for the fans of a versatile writer. For example, a publisher decided that a bestselling historical romance writer was unmarketable as a contemporary romance writer and wouldn't accept the book she turned in (which she then sold elsewhere, fortunately). Another example: A successful fantasy writer's mainstream historical novel didn't get marketed to fantasy readers, because the publisher's marketing department believed that the author's audience would not be interested in a novel which was not in exactly the same sub-sub-category.

Nowhere is the pressure to fit into an extant marketing niche more keenly felt by writers than in romance, possibly the most market-driven of the genres (being the most popular and therefore the most lucrative). This has created some confusion within the genre as various writers attempt to write outside of the extant market definitions of romance, generating discussion about what is romance, what is romantic women's fiction, what is mainstream women's fiction, and so on.

I think the discussion is healthy for the marketplace, as long as it doesn't get unhealthy for writers—i.e. people mistakenly assuming that fitting within extant market definitions identifies themselves, or others, as "lesser" writers. Good grief. If this is your secret shoulder chip, get over it.

Read my lips: The marketing parameters of a book are not

an indicator of its quality. They're simply part of the overall societal trend to define something as specifically (or narrowly) as possible in order to sell it.

And since art is subjective, bookstores can't organize their stock under user-friendly banners like "Excellent Books," "Mediocre Generic Books," and "Really Bad Books That We Can't Believe Anyone Published." It would be convenient in theory, but it would never work in practice, since one reader's favorite novel is the same book that another reader gives to her dog as a chew toy. Consequently, instead, we get the sub-sub-categorization ("a Regency-era paranormal time-travel historical romance"), and the "a novel in the tradition of" marketing schemes, and the "why can't you write a book like so-and-so?" editorial comments (which, yes, I and several of my acquaintances have all had, word for word). This is how publishers, like almost all other businesses marketing products to the modern American consumer, attempt to stake out their audiences and claim the Yankee dollar.

So if your work doesn't fit into an extant marketing category, what can you do? Actually, there are many options: Wait for the market to change; it often does. (I've recently sold a new series that fits the current marketplace well, but which was "unmarketable" when I first wrote and submitted it years ago.) Sell to a small press that believes in the work (which I did with *Fallen From Grace*, a book which then became my first-ever finalist for the prestigious Rita Award). Self-publish (can you say *"The Celestine Prophecy"*?). Work toward name-recognition with more commercial material, then present your "unmarket-able" book when a publisher will buy something just because you're the author; it's a long-range plan which has worked for some writers. Attempt to revise the work so that it retains the essential features which matter most to you, but within a more marketable framework.

Or find a good agent who believes in the work and can find a major publisher who believes in it, too. Become that blockbuster success story who invents a new commercial trend and is imitated by other writers and publishers. As *New York Times* bestselling novelist Jayne Ann Krentz has said any number of times, the new trends in commercial fiction come from authors, not publishers, editors, or agents.

So go forth and conquer. Hell, *someone* has to do it—why not you?

It Can Happen Here—
And Often Does

I once attended a community theatre production of *The Importance of Being Ernest* which lives vibrantly in my memory because, somewhere in Act Two, the entire set collapsed, fell on the actors, and attacked the audience with flying debris.

This livened up an otherwise dull evening.

Of course, live theatre is rich with anecdotes of things that go wrong in the middle of performances. I once read an account of a restaurant delivery boy who saw a horrified expression cross Paul Newman's face as the unwitting lad announced to him that his food had arrived...while Newman was in the middle of a matinee performance on Broadway. When the actor playing Tony in a regional production of *West Side Story* softly crooned the lyrics "the most beautiful sound I ever heard...," the hushed theatre was suddenly filled with the thundering crash of a toolbox falling off the catwalk. British actor Antony Sher's Achilles tendon snapped in the middle of a performance of *King Lear*. Speaking of Shakespeare, an actor playing *Richard III* in Poland died when one of his fellow actors accidentally stabbed him for real in Act Five.

So, you see, there's an even tougher profession than writing.

Relatively few of the gaffs and disasters of the publishing business actually happen to writers before a live audience, thank goodness, but we nonetheless get waylaid by our industry's own hair-tearing brand of bizarre mix-ups, infuriating screw-ups, and wacky mistakes that are out of the writer's control.

Let's start with names. Don't you just hate it when they get your name wrong? My name was misspelled two different ways (Resnich and Resnik) on one sole page of my publisher's sales catalog one season.

"The very first byline I ever got in a real press read 'Joan Yolen,'" says Jane Yolen. Another science fiction/fantasy writer recounts, "One of my novelizations was supposed to come out under a pseudonym, but the publisher 'forgot' and used my real name." This also happened to romance writer Jo Ann Ferguson (and the novel came out simultaneously with a novella which *was* published under her pseudonym). Katharine Eliska Kimbriel's name was misspelled on the title page (the only page she didn't get to proofread in galleys) of *Hidden Fires*. Doranna Durgin's name was also misspelled on the title page of a novel. Lillian Stewart Carl's name was misspelled in a *Locus* ad. Vonda McIntyre's name is misspelled on the spine of the Science Fiction Book Club edition of her first novel, *The Exile Waiting*. J. Ardian Lee's first novel in Germany was copyrighted under the wrong name. When the producer of the ABC TV movie *Volcano: Fire on the Mountain* insisted to scriptwriter (and mystery novelist) Steven Womack that leaving the "n" off his first name in the title credits was no big deal, Womack replied,

"Good thing you guys didn't produce *The Godfather*. Otherwise, it would've starred Marlo Brando."

Nor is it only the *author's* name which publishers get wrong. Romance writer Anne Stuart notes that the protagonist's name was misspelled in the back cover copy of her fifth novel. And sometimes it's not the *publisher* that gets your name wrong: Cheryl Anne Porter once showed up at a signing to discover that, instead of her new romance novel, the bookstore had unwittingly ordered *Gross Grub!* by Cheryl Porter, a children's writer.

Still on the subject of names, romance writer Suzanne Simmons' name was simply left *off* the cover of her first novel: "Just a blank space where my name should have been. Once I got over the disappointment, I had to laugh. It's turned out to be excellent training for the bizarre and sometimes inexplicable world of publishing."

What could be as bad (I hear you ask) as having your name left off your book's cover? How about seeing your name on someone *else's* book? Amazon.com erroneously listed me as co-author of all of David Coe's fantasy novels. (I naturally contacted David and demanded half of all his earnings.) Romance writer Annette Mahon reports, "One of my books had my cover and my title page...but everything else in it was someone else's book." Another writer once showed up at a signing to discover that, on a portion of the print run, her name and title had been slapped on some other writer's book. Conversely, a romance novel by Judy Gill was once released with someone else's cover on it.

Sometimes your name and cover appear on a novel that turns out to be only *partly* your own. Romance writer Becky Barker once found a portion of another writer's novel in the middle of hers, for part of the print run. Yet another writer reports finding forty pages of a horror novel bound into about two thousand copies of her historical romance. About halfway through the original edition of Patricia Matthews' first science fiction/fantasy novel, *The Other People*, the reader was suddenly thrust into the Old West, with cowboys, cattle, and shooting. No one found this more surprising than the author herself. By coincidence, a friend of hers under contract to the same publisher discovered "vampires, werewolves, and assorted odd people" stuck in the middle of his newly published novel about the Old West. There'd been a mix-up with the manuscripts when the books were printed. Fortunately for the writers, the publisher chose to go back to press and get correct versions of both novels into the marketplace. Meanwhile, editor Denise Little recalls the time that some pages from *Penthouse Magazine* accidentally got inserted (you should pardon the expression) between the covers of a Disney book. Now there's a twist on sex education that could make Minnie Mouse wake up screaming.

However, these examples notwithstanding, you may well be the author of everything between the covers of your book...as well as the material that got left out. My copy of *Asimov's Guide To the Bible* is missing about forty pages in the middle. A fantasy writer I know says her publisher dropped the final three chapters from one of her books. She only discovered this when they delivered the galleys so late that they claimed there was no time to do anything about the missing chapters. Vonda McIntyre says that a Swedish publisher left out the last chapter of *Dreamsnake*. She adds, "*Dreamsnake* is a very existential book without the last chapter." (Since the last chapter was Chapter 13, McIntyre thinks maybe the editor was triskaidekaphobic.) Denise Little was managing a bookstore in Texas when James Michener's *Texas* was released. The store sold four thousand hardcover copies of the novel before discovering that their entire shipment was defective: sixty-four pages were missing from the middle of the book. (Strangely, only four customers ever returned their copies.)

The worst example of missing pages may come from a writer who sold her first novel to a little-known Kensington imprint called Precious Gems. When her advance copies arrived, she discovered that some ten thousand words were haphazardly chopped out of the book *after* she had proofread the galleys. "When I called my editor, deliriously angry, she told me that Precious Gems had changed the standard word-count for the imprint some four hours before my book was printed." So the editor simply went through the manuscript making random cuts without notifying the author then or later.

Even when all the words are there, though, the book may still not be the one you expected to get. Three chapters of a Judy Gill novel were published upside down. The pages were out of order in part of the print run of a novel by Madeline Baker. Another writer's book was released with dozens of typos on every page when the printer received the wrong computer file.

And those are all just examples of what can go wrong on the *inside* of a published book. Back when I was romance novelist Laura Leone, I once got a cover so bad that my editor wouldn't show it to me until I was safely eight hundred miles away from her. (It was baaaaaad—and the book earned less than any other romance novel I ever wrote.) Kensington once released a romance novel with an elaborately embossed and flocked cover which might have been a winner...except that the flocking wore off during shipping; so when it arrived in stores, the female cover model's breasts looked naked. (Explanation for the men in our audience: This look doesn't attract women readers.) Through some mysterious oversight, the cover of a Christina Dodd romance novel portrayed a heroine with three arms. Novelist Katie Daniel was asked to revise a character's physical description after the wrong model showed up for the cover shoot. When Vonda McIntyre asked to see the Dutch cover of *Dreamsnake*, her Dutch editor said, "I'll show it to you only if you promise not to kill me." McIntyre saw the cover and says, "I tried to kill him."

Speaking of murder and mayhem, the IRS terrorized writer Pat Rice when a publisher's accounting department wildly misreported her income. The confusion resulted from the accounting department having spent much of the year sending checks for the wrong amounts and also sending checks to the wrong address while Rice struggled valiantly to get accurate sums delivered to the right address. In an equally convoluted mix-up, a science fiction/fantasy writer reports being contracted to create an entire tie-in series for an agent/packager who, it was later revealed, didn't actually have the rights to the project. So the writer had wasted all the work she'd already invested in planning the series and writing several chapters of the first book.

On a darker note, U.S. book sales nosedived immediately following the terrorist attacks of September 11, 2001. Major media appearances were cancelled, blockbuster releases went unnoticed, sell-throughs were abysmal, and midlist novelists came close to standing on street corners with signs saying, "Will write for food." Book sales took a similar plunge a decade earlier, during the First Gulf War. Denise Little, who was a mass market buyer for Barnes & Noble before moving over to the dark side (i.e. becoming an editor) advises writers whose sales records are hurt by such catastrophic events to chart their releases against a calendar so that, in future negotiations, they can convincingly demonstrate that their terrible sales in that instance had absolutely nothing to do with their overall career patterns.

Finally, I have saved the best for last. Remember Kensington's previously mentioned romance imprint, Precious Gems, where a writer woke up one day to find ten thousand words missing from her published novel? Another Precious Gems writer has an even better (or, rather, worse) tale to tell. Trish Jensen, writing under the pseudonym Trish Graves, sold them a novel called *Just This Once* in which the hero, among other things, mentors a teenage boy, steering him away from street gangs and toward organized sports. So you may imagine the author's shock when, upon reading her galleys, she discovered that the editor had changed the boy into a raccoon.

(I think I speak for everyone here when I say, "*What?*")

When Jensen asked the editor why on earth she had rewritten a teenager as a small nocturnal carnivore, the editor replied that the hero's mentoring the boy could be misconstrued as having undertones of pedophilia. (All together now: "*Huh?*") So the obvious solution was to rewrite the kid as an animal.

I am not making this up.

Jensen says, "I screamed to high heaven, my agent screamed to high heaven. We wanted the book pulled. Kensington said it was too late. They couldn't pull it, and it was too late to turn it back into what it had been." Understandably, she adds, "I was heartsick for a long time. To this day I can't look at that book."

The lesson here is that when you allow an editor absolute

control over your work, as that Precious Gems contract stipulated, the results can be worse than your wildest nightmares. Jensen made sure her next contract with Kensington didn't have that clause, and she warned other Precious Gems writers about it, too. She's wryly philosophical about the experience these days, saying, "Now I'm known as 'the raccoon author.'"

As for Precious Gems, the imprint no longer exists. It folded within a few years of the raccoon episode. A rare example of things turning out as they should in the publishing industry.

Nurturing the Nature

Maybe an Amazon reader has compared your new novel to rancid pork. Possibly someone at *Publisher's Weekly* has written a review of your work that seems like a personal vendetta. Or perhaps nine editors in a row have rejected your latest manuscript. Perchance your agent has snorted the entire agency, as well as six months' worth of your earnings, up his nose, or fled the country with his much-younger male secretary while your career is at a crucial juncture. Or perhaps your editor has sent you a fifteen-page, single-spaced letter demanding revisions which you defy her to characterize as "reasonable" while keeping a straight face. Maybe your publisher isn't paying your fall royalties until winter, and they're openly annoyed that you *mind* being paid months late.

Has a major retailer refused to carry your new book because they dislike the cover that your publisher has put on it? (And has your publisher then, in a fit of stereotypical predictability, abandoned both you and the book?) Have you gotten a cover with copy for the wrong novel on it? Has an editor rewritten one of your characters as a raccoon? Has your hard drive crashed in the middle of a deadline, or your printer died while printing an overdue manuscript? Have you woken up to find out your editor has been laid off, your imprint has been discontinued, or your publisher has folded?

Heigh ho, the glamorous life of the working novelist!

And in the ceaseless hail of the publishing world's slings and arrows, you have to keep writing. Without a full creative well and the mental focus needed to craft riveting fiction, we cannot survive professionally as novelists. Yet the publishing industry, the marketplace, the logistics of the work, and even life itself regularly intrude on the paradise of the imagination, turning it into a desert.

So how do novelists keep fertilizing the soil? How do you nurture your creative nature and comfort yourself as a writer swinging in the breeze of this brutal profession?

"Food," says novelist Patricia Bray. "Food is good. Chocolate and alcohol are better." Silhouette writer Katherine Garbera recommends Krispy Kreme doughnuts. Novelist Tracy Grant advises, "Keep good single malt whiskey and French champagne on hand." Jodie Larsen Nida recommends a frozen strawberry daiquiri in the shade in summer, and adds, "No matter what the season, French Vanilla or Toasted Marshmallow Jelly Bellies are my favorite reward! What could be better than sweet treats that have only four calories apiece?" Personally, when stuck in morbid distraction while my bank account dwindles into negative figures because it takes five months for a check to travel from New York to Cincinnati, I find solace in the Elizabeth Bevarly Theory of Plotting: There is no plot problem that cookies cannot solve.

Longtime novelist Barbara Keiler says, "I've endured times

when the only nurturing which seems to work involves chocolate consumption." (Let the church say, "Amen!") However, she
neatly counters the inevitable consequences of chocolate consumption with jogging. Having commenced with brisk walking,
Keiler eventually worked up to a slow, steady, daily jog of about
five miles, and she says, "[It] has worked wonders for me. It
eases stress, increases my energy level, gets me pumped up, and
helps me empty the 'trash' in my brain...And since the brain
abhors a vacuum, once I empty the 'trash,' the useful thoughts
come rushing in." [Resnick, who also hates vacuuming, briefly
considers jogging...but soon regains her senses and re-embraces
the Elizabeth Bevarly Theory of Plotting.]

Katherine Garbera admits she hates to exercise but
nonetheless says, "Yoga helps to make everything flow together
for me." She finds that yoga in the morning is a great way to
start the writing day. I myself am giving yoga a whirl at the
local yoga school. I like the lying-on-the-floor-and-dozing part
of it, but I'm having trouble adjusting to the "now lift every bit
of your body except your left elbow off the floor" portion of it.
However, while yoga has not yet filled me with story solutions,
it has become an asset in stress management.

Writer Annette Mahon suggests an additional (and less
acrobatic) way to nurture the writer by caring for the body:
She pays a professional massage therapist to come to her house
and give her an upper body massage once every two weeks.
"It makes *such* a difference to the neck, back, and shoulders.
I especially have problems with my right shoulder—that
darn mouse!—and it feels wonderful for almost a week after
[the masseuse's] visits." In addition to massage, Tracy Grant
recommends facials. Jodie Larsen Nida enjoys "a long rest in
the whirlpool with the jets hitting my tired neck and shoulder

muscles." I like a hot, scented bath, a glass of wine, candles, and a good audiobook to listen to while I relax.

Shopping is another popular way we take care of ourselves. (Of course, "shopping" presupposes that your check has made the arduous, months-long, overland journey from New York City to your mailbox.) Katherine Garbera tries to buy something little with each new sale or success she has. Bestseller Barbara Samuel goes to a tourist town she has loved since childhood and buys baubles like copper bracelets and faux turquoise. I like to buy books (and, come on, is there anyone here who *doesn't*?). Tracy Grant buys cute "writing clothes" and Victoria's Secret pajamas rather than just working in old sweats. In fact, I started doing this several years ago, too, and have found it picks me up on low days. Sitting here in pretty loungewear costs no more than my sweats, and it feels nicer.

Cynthia Pratt stresses that she goes shopping by herself, particularly when stuck on some point in her work, to steep herself in sights, smells, textures—and other people's conversations. "Just getting out among 'normal folks' is a great creativity generator." Indeed, "getting out," in one way or another, is a common means of nurturing ourselves—undoubtedly because we spend so much time cooped up alone in a little room with only our imagination for company.

"I go to the pub and drink Guinness with my girlfriends and listen to a Celtic band play badly," says Barbara Samuel. Silhouette author Ann Schuessler might meet a friend for coffee, spend time at a new art exhibit, visit a museum, see a play, or attend the opera. Patricia Bray greets rejection letters the same way she celebrates writing successes: by going out to dinner with someone she enjoys talking to. Writer Nancy Cohen will call someone she hasn't spoken to in a while or "just go out to have fun." Although there are times in a writing schedule or in the creative process when I need isolation, I don't thrive well for long without regular contact with the people whose love supports me, whose wit stimulates me, and whose wisdom enriches me; so I make sure I spend time with my friends. I also enjoy spending time at our wonderful local zoo, where every day feels likes a holiday.

My single favorite way of nurturing myself is a popular one among writers: travel. Sue-Ellen Welfonder, who writes Scottish medieval romances, makes two trips per year to Scotland to "spend weeks driving all by myself through the Highlands, seeking out the most remote and atmospheric places I can find. Each trip replenishes my soul and my creative well, while the anticipation of the next one keeps me going when I am here." When feeling depressed or stressed, Welfonder places her airline ticket for her next Scottish trip in a visible spot on her desk. "Just seeing it lying there warms my heart and makes me smile." Novelist Evelyn Rogers leaves the country if she can afford it, usually on low-budget trips to Europe, preferably Italy: "There's nothing like wine sipped in a palazzo to revive the spirits." Barbara Samuel describes herself as "addicted to travel" and delighted by the myriad details she finds in new places. She rhapsodizes about how tickled she was to see dew so heavy "it *dripped* off the trees" when she was here in Cincinnati last year. (Our sodden climate is one of the reasons we Cincinnatians are also addicted to travel.) Upon experiencing a burnout so thorough that I wanted to quit writing, I abandoned my career and spent a year crossing Africa. I've written over a million words since then, so I guess it revived me.

However, not all solutions to creative desertification need

involve airfare and yellow fever shots. Cindi Myers, using an idea she got from *Write It Down, Make It Happen* by Henriette Anne Klauser, collects compliments: "I keep a little notebook, and into it goes copies of fan letters, any encouraging comments I've gotten about my work or myself as a person, favorite quotes, anecdotes, etc." I keep notebooks filled with things that have made me look twice or start dreaming: magazine pictures, postcards, stickers, stamps, maps, favorite poems, favorite song lyrics, favorite quotes, bizarre news items, amusing articles, notes on interesting traditional weapons, possible titles, possible story ideas, special mementos. When I open these notebooks, I again feel the infinite creative possibilities of their contents.

For another stay-at-home stimulation to creativity, novelist Lillian Stewart Carl recommends crossword puzzles: "The effort it takes me to find the word that fits the clue is just enough to turn off that hyperactive leaping-around of the thought processes and help me either to calm down or focus, depending on what my goal is." Writer Cheryl Wolverton goes to the movies or reads outside of her genre, "so I can allow fresh ideas from different perspectives to fill me when I'm running on empty." Tina Wainscott cherishes the rare treat of "getting to *read*" something that is just for fun and has nothing to do with her work in progress. Romance novelist Toni Blake says she takes a nap or reads a book if she feels like it, even if she should be writing at the time, adding, "I just generally try to be good to myself when possible, figuring I'm a lot more likely to turn out good writing if I'm feeling happy and content."

In fact, the practice of being good to oneself is a powerful fortress against any siege on a writer's creative health. Sue-Ellen Welfonder steers clear of "those online romance sites I know to be of the slash-and-burn variety. Nor do I skim reader message boards…Since I went cold turkey on those things about a year ago, my nerves have vastly improved." She also writes more since then. Ann Schuessler tries not to compare her own career with her friends': "We are each on our own path, and as long as I remember that, I'm okay." When she forgets that, she makes herself miserable.

Thriller writer Ronn Kaiser wisely tries to put his failures, setbacks, and problems from his mind, because embracing them is self-defeating. He believes that creative behavior is natural and instinctual, and that inhibitions are the construct. So, he says, "If, as I believe, I am but a conduit for the creative forces in the ether, then work isn't about me, it's about process and product…which means the name of the game is turning off the ego and letting the powers of the universe flow into me and through me." I myself find that if I praise myself for how much I'm getting done rather than condemn myself for how much I'm not getting done, I get more done. It's not just perspective, I actually do accomplish more work this way.

Additionally, trust in ourselves and respect for our work is vital nourishment for our creativity. After more than twenty years in this profession, bestselling novelist Kay Hooper has learned "not to waste time or energy, or lose sleep, whenever I run headlong into that inevitable wall in whatever book I'm working on." Kay looks at the long line of books on the nearby wall with her name on them and reminds herself that she *does* know how to do this. Then she turns her computer off and walks away. She gets on with her life, takes the time she needs, doesn't let herself drown in guilt about it, and doesn't return to the book "until I have that—also inevitable—moment of realization: 'Oh, yeah—that's what I need to do!'" The real comfort, Kay says, is that she has finally learned to trust herself and her abilities.

When Cheryl Wolverton receives rejections or bad news, she says, "I have to remind myself that I am doing this for me." Cynthia Pratt finds it helpful "to remind myself every so often that I am extremely lucky not to be standing behind a counter or a broom—which usually suffices to send me back to my chair with renewed determination." Remembering some of my own past jobs (kennel girl, cleaning lady, waitress, cashier, office temp, telemarketer, ale wench, dishwasher) is a pretty reliable way for me to start feeling remarkably lucky and terribly creative again.

Finally, a means of nurturing ourselves as writers which novelist Judy Gill mentions: "You know what gives me a bigger high than anything else in this world? Writing. Just sitting down and writing and leaving my desk at the end of the day wonderfully exhausted but supremely satisfied deep in my soul. Oh, yeah...and then there's chocolate."

Those Who Are About to Reboot, We Salute You!

One November, my agent casually asked if it was going to cause a tax glitch for me that, due to our having made a sale at the start of the month, I'd be getting a signing check right before the end of the year. I, of course, laughed gaily at this naïve question. (Okay, "gaily" might be hyperbole.) All my previous experience with the publishing house in question had consistently proven that there was no possibility whatsoever of my receiving the *contract* in as little as eight weeks, never mind the first check.

Anyhow, if there *had* been a snowball's chance in hell of my getting paid in December, that money would have come in handy at the time. While I was trying to print the final manuscript of the book for which I had not yet received a contract, my trusty old Brother printer died. This was a sentimental blow to me, as I had enjoyed that printer for its eccentricity. The first time it ever broke down and I called tech support for help, the young man on the other end of the phone line instructed me to clear the surface of my desk, turn the printer upside down, and bang it hard against the desk three times.

They just don't make 'em like that anymore.

So I was sad to lose the Brother; but I had known this day was coming. The thing was seven years old, and no one lives forever. Besides, after getting the bill for its repair some three years earlier, I'd discovered that it had cost me more to fix it than it would have cost me to replace it. Moreover, the repair shop had inflicted on me all that familiar, dreaded, techno-dweeb hemming and hawing about how this printer was so old that they'd have to cobble together repair parts out of forgotten Cold War refuse from nuclear waste dumps in Siberia and then transport it to an old blind monk in the hills who was the last person in this hemisphere with the arcane knowledge needed to repair a machine this obsolete.

You know the spiel.

And that was three whole years ago. That's twenty-one dog years. In computer terms, it's about nine centuries. In other words, by that December, it would have been easier to find Osama Bin Laden's jock strap than it was to find the right parts to repair my comatose printer. (Whereas it remains quite easy to get my ancient Toyota repaired, and my bedside lamp is older than my parents.)

Where was I?

Oh, yes. So I went out looking for a new printer. I *hate* shopping for new equipment. I've been stringing wires together and reading instruction manuals non-stop since 1988, and I'm tired of it. But a working writer needs a printer; especially a working writer who'd like to deliver a book and get paid for it, oh, five months later.

Well, here's the interesting thing I discovered upon

shopping for a new printer: I couldn't *use* a new printer with
my computer. Brace yourself for some technical jargon: The
printer port (i.e. the socket where you plug in the printer) on
my computer was a "serial port." About two years earlier, the
entire industry had come up with the bright idea of ceasing all
production and sales of serial port printers. Ever since then,
printers must be plugged into a "USB port."

In other words, the bastards changed the shape of the plugs.

Now maybe this is old news to you, and you're astonished
that I'm so out-of-touch and anachronistic that I was out there
shopping for a serial port printer; but I, for one, was shocked
to find that everywhere I went, the best advice any computer
stores could give me was that I should spend $900-$3,400 on a
new computer to solve the problem of the damn plug on all the
damn printers manufactured for the previous two years being
incompatible with all the damn sockets they made on computers before that.

This is organized crime at its finest.

Needless to say, I decided to look for an alternative to
dropping $900-$3,400 on impulse, despite the blank stares
that my questions about a possible alternative produced at
every computer store I entered. Okay, sure, I found the shaking heads and long, negative, incomprehensible replies a bit
discouraging; but I'm a *writer*—I eat discouraging obstacles and
idiotic responses for breakfast!

Moreover, my determination to solve the problem without
buying a new computer tripled after I learned that I'd need to
spend even *more* money if I actually wanted to *work* on a new
computer. This is because the industry has ensured that the
newest operating systems cannot run the majority of the software produced before last week; ergo, if I bought a new system,

I'd have to buy new software in order to open and print the manuscript for which I had initially gone forth in search of a new printer. And the price of such software is roughly what I paid for my car (a car for which—did I mention this?—I can still readily find spare parts).

So, due to the computer industry ensuring instant obsolescence of everything it sells us, I could only replace my $300 printer by first spending a fortune on hardware and software.

These people will soon form their own Reich and start bombing Poland.

This is why the average working writer needs a secret army of computer-geek friends. Mine all happen to belong to the Cincinnati Fantasy Group (CFG), one of the oldest clubs in science fiction/fantasy fandom. I consulted Scott Street (the club's webmaster), Stephen Leigh (a novelist), and Frank Johnson (a disc jockey), all of whom have kept me from shooting the computer on several occasions. Finally, Guy Allen (engineer and, more importantly, host of the famous annual Chili Con) walked me through the exact steps I needed to solve my problem.

This is how I—yes, I—wound up installing hardware. It turned out that for a total cost of about fifty dollars, I could take my computer apart, install a "USB port," install the "driver" to make the port work, install the operating system upgrade to make the driver work, and *then* go shop for a new printer. So that's exactly what I did.

I'll bet you're impressed.

I'll bet you're also wondering why none of the many computer industry employees I'd talked to had ever said to me, "Oh, sure, you can solve this problem by spending about fifty dollars and an hour of your time."

Have I mentioned the three full days I wasted running around to computer stores asking for help?

Why, I keep asking myself, does someone like me even *need* to learn to install hardware?

Oh, wait, now I remember. It's because the computer industry is run by pirates, rapists, and thieves, that's why.

Oh, well. As they say, all good things come to an end…and my computer turned out to be one of them. About three months after my hunt for a printer, my computer started making noises like a lawn mower preparing to blow up. It was five years old, and no computer lives forever…or even as long as a good pair of shoes. One day, it gave up the ghost and went silent.

This happened less than five months after I'd printed and shipped that book, so, of course, I hadn't been paid the delivery check yet. And while looking at the migraine-inducing prices on new computers and new software, I got some shocking news from the IRS; the previous year certainly hadn't *felt* like a good one, but my tax statements showed otherwise, and the IRS wanted even more blood than they'd already drained from me.

I retreated into a morbid depression during which I watched about twenty episodes of *Trading Spaces* and made a dent in Ohio's supply of Ben & Jerry's Ice Cream.

A couple of weeks later, my new computer arrived. The first thing I noticed was that I couldn't attach it to my trusty old 17" monitor because (wait for it!) the bastards had changed the shape of the plugs.

I wasted two more full days running all over town asking for an adapter. "I cannot," I kept saying to blank-faced, head-shaking computer store employees, "be the only person who ever bought a new computer while still owning a perfectly good old monitor. Other people on this planet besides me must have wanted an adapter."

"Maybe so," these fellows all replied...but that didn't change the fact that the only possible solution to my problem (they insisted) was to spend $300-$1,900 on a new monitor.

Even *remembering* this makes my skull feel like exploding and painting their faces in splattered schmutz. (Sorry about the imagery.)

Finally, at the suggestion of one of my friendly CFG gurus, I contacted a local store called Computer DNA. They instantly said, sure, they had an adapter, come on over and get it. The actual price was fifteen dollars, but since they'd quoted ten dollars to me on the phone, they only charged me ten dollars.

So I was wrong! Not *all* computer industry people are the minions of Beelzebub! Some of them (i.e. the tiny handful of people working at Computer DNA) are even terrific folks.

Next up, I had to find an adapter for my keyboard, because (you can see it coming, can't you?) the bastards had changed the shape of the plugs.

Then, with my hardware problems finally solved, I turned my attention to my software problems.

The only version of my email program which worked with the new operating system wouldn't read the earlier version in which all my contact addresses were stored. My screensaver program, to which I was deeply attached (a series of "tropical paradise" pictures that I stare at when stuck for the next sentence), not only wouldn't work with the new operating system, it even (inexplicably) made the CD drive malfunction for a full day after I tried to install it. The only versions of any word processing software that worked with the new operating system could not communicate with Alphasmart, the mercifully simple word processor on which I'd been writing while awaiting the arrival of the new computer.

By the time the Alphasmart tech support people heard from me, I was weeping tears of exhaustion. I was also terrified into near-hysteria that I wasn't going to be able to transfer a week's worth of work from the Alphasmart to the computer. The nice man at Alphasmart talked me down from the ledge, then solved my problem. This involved choosing a different "start-up disk" on the computer, rebooting into an older version of the operating system, opening an older version of a word processing program, connecting the Alphasmart to that for uploading, then saving and closing the word processing document, choosing a different start-up disk again, rebooting back to the new operating system, and then using the newest word processing software to open the saved document.

I am not making this up.

Once my software problems were also solved (or else, in some cases, abandoned as lost causes), I began working my way through two expensive instruction manuals (one of them more than 800 pages long) which I bought to help me figure out how to use the operating system, which is five years newer than my previous one. That translates into thirty-five dog years, or seventy-nine generations of computer hardware and software upgrades.

At some point in my adventures with the helpful technological tools of the modern novelist, I may even find the time to write again.

Vive La France!

January 11. The day I finally lose my mind.

I don't just have a hallucinatory episode. I don't just feel dizzy with frustration. I don't just want to hit myself in the head with a brick until I pass out and no longer have to endure the day. No, this time, I finally lose my mind.

Of course, it's no secret that I killed a lot of brain cells writing my last book. People say it's drink, drugs, fornication, and loud rock 'n' roll music that destroys your mind, but I know better. I survived all those things (and many more) with my wits intact (relatively speaking).

True, writing my last novel sent me close to the edge. Too close, I admit. Back when I was working on that interminable project, I would dream, once every few months, that I had finished it. I would dream writing the final scene, writing the words "The End," printing the manuscript, packing it, shipping it, and telling my agent and my editor that it was finally done.

I would dream this, enter a state of euphoric happiness…and

then wake up and realize it was only a dream, and I still had hundreds of pages left to write.

You can perhaps imagine how hard it was to get out of bed on such mornings.

So, sure, writing that book burned me out, took me down for the count, and caused muscles in my back to knot up which have yet to unknot. Yes, I did indeed kill a few brain cells working on that monster.

But I didn't actually lose my mind. Not then. Not until later. It isn't the writing itself, but rather the writing life that has finally done me in.

January 11. The day they finally drive me out of my mind.

My God, I think, I want to go back to France and hide there forever.

※

It was called Utopia, and aptly named. It was a pan-European science fiction/fantasy convention funded by European Union money and held in November. I don't know exactly how many people attended, though it was clearly several thousand. We were in Nantes, a small city in France. Close to the western Loire Valley, with its vineyards and chateaux. Equally close to the Atlantic coast and the famous megalithic monuments of Brittany.

They brought in writers from all over, including Russia and the Americas. I was one of half a dozen U.S. writers there, my airfare from America and my train fare from Paris paid for by the committee. They put me up for five nights in a hotel next to the convention center. Complimentary breakfast in the hotel's restaurant was included every day. On the second floor of the convention center was a private club room for writers and other VIPs, with an open bar. Local wine, hard cider, café au lait, whatever. All free. All served by a good-looking young bartender who told me what was good and what wasn't each day, since the red wine wasn't always up to his high standards.

(Here in the U.S., I am accustomed to getting one free-drink chit at the start of the World Science Fiction Convention for the annual, sardine-packed, poorly-ventilated "Meet the Pros" party. The idea is that writers will show up if we're promised one free drink, and fans theoretically come to the party in hopes of meeting us. In reality, I've seen so few fans at these events that I suspect they all know better than to get between a writer and a free drink. By the time I arrive each year, though, there's seldom anything left but some warm yellow soda that I suspect will kill me if I ever actually drink it.)

On the third floor of the Nantes convention center was a restaurant. Complimentary lunch and dinner each day for writers and other VIPs. At home, I am accustomed to the word "writer" being linked with "unemployable scum of the earth" rather than with "VIPs," and so I was initially sure that I wouldn't be welcome in the VIP restaurant. However, Hugo Award-winning editor Gardner Dozois assured me that he had been there himself and had seen other writers (even other American writers) there, and I would not be thrown out. So I went upstairs and cautiously gave my real name at the door. And it worked! They fed me! Every day!

In exchange for all this largesse, I was expected to do only one thing: appear on one panel with a few other writers.

Nothing more. However...it turned out that the transportation coordinator managed to book me on a train back to Paris several hours before my panel was scheduled.

This didn't really surprise me, as it was very consistent with the rest of my dealings with Myriam, the transportation coordinator (who was evidently an employee of the city of Nantes rather than a member of the convention committee). Myriam had managed to book other people on flights that didn't exist, and to book me on additional flights that I hadn't requested and didn't want. At one point, Myriam refused to provide me with a confirmation number or with tickets, and insisted the airline was mistaken when they said there was no reservation for me and no way I would be allowed on the plane. It wasn't until eighteen hours before my departure that I finally convinced Myriam to tell me which hotel I was booked into. When I asked for an address and for directions, she e-mailed me that upon emerging from the Nantes train station, I would see the hotel, which I could easily walk to.

She neglected to mention that there was a large body of water between the train station and the hotel, and no direct means of getting from one place to the other.

Actually, even before learning of the scheduling gaff, I had already asked Myriam to change my train ticket for me, since she had scheduled it without consulting me and it wasn't the departure time I wanted. She, the travel coordinator, told me that changing my ticket would be too much trouble for her. She added that I would have no problem changing it myself after I arrived in Nantes. I merely had to walk (read: swim) to the train station and request the switch.

Myriam also neglected to mention that it was a holiday weekend in France and that I was returning to Paris on one of the busiest travel days of the year. The clerk at the train station actually laughed aloud when I told him I wanted to change my ticket.

I made my way back to the convention center (via the circuitous pedestrian route I had eventually discovered, which enabled me to avoid swimming there) and informed the programming chair that—after they'd provided me with airfare, train fare, hotel, and meals—I wouldn't be able to do the one sole thing they had expected of me in exchange, because my train departed four hours before my panel began.

He shrugged, smiled, and asked in detail how I was enjoying the conference.

Myriam notwithstanding, I never wanted to come home.

❄

Right before I left for my all-expenses-paid trip to Europe, I got fired from a work-for-hire project which I had thought would pay some of the bills which had managed to accumulate in a looming mountain while I was writing a 1,732-page fantasy novel. So suddenly this income isn't coming in, after all. Oops. However, I tell myself consolingly, delivery money for my obese fantasy opus will surely roll in soon. After all, my editor reportedly loves the book, and my agent believes this matter will be wrapped up by the end of the year. What could go wrong?

Rhetorical question, of course.

Thanksgiving comes and goes with no money. Then Christmas comes and goes with no money, as does the New Year. I plead with my agent, who in turn nags my publisher. Things get grim. I get down to my last few dollars in the world, while simultaneously producing so much material that I find recent documents on my hard drive that I don't even remember having written.

As exhaustion consumes me and my cash flow dries up, I think about how much I want to go back to France and hide there forever.

✳

Did I mention the food?

This wasn't the usual congealed conference slop which has given me a lifelong horror of fluorescent lighting and round dinner tables. No, indeed! The VIP restaurant consisted of hot and cold buffet tables groaning under the immense weight of endless quantities of food so delicious it makes me weep to remember it. There are roughly four hundred varieties of cheese in France, and the most exquisite examples of them were there—served exactly at room temperature, along with ripe fruit and a selection of tasty biscuits and crackers. The dessert table was magnificent enough to inspire symphonies, and its *pièce de résistance* was "floating isles," a dish of whipped egg-white islands in a custard sauce that almost made me beg to have the chef's love-child. The hot entrees and side dishes offered so many mouth-watering choices that I never got to try them all, no matter how gluttonous I was.

Which is not to say that we always ate in the VIP restaurant. They served us food elsewhere, too. The opening-night party took place in a vast hall where handsome waiters kept refilling my glass with French champagne while I wandered among table after table after table of seafood appetizers. Oysters so fresh they needed only a little squeeze of lemon juice to make them perfect, plump jumbo shrimp, amazing little caviar *hors d'oeuvres*...A person could get used to living like that.

On another occasion, they hosted a four-course meal for us at the city's gorgeous art museum, where we dined beneath chandeliers dripping with crystal. Prior to the meal, just in case we needed entertainment, there was a guide to walk us through the new Picasso exhibit. (Almost spoiled my appetite. I hate Picasso. All those chopped up women.)

Lest we bruise our little feet with walking, there were also hired cars at our beck and call.

*

Back home in the States, I finally receive word that my check has arrived at my agency and will be here within a few days. I almost keel over with relief, then go back to searching the couch cushions for enough spare change to buy milk.

Really, I tell myself, things will be fine now. I'm due a short story check, a check for my monthly column, and money for the book I delivered months ago. All expected to arrive in the coming week. My worst troubles are over. Happy days are here again. In a few days, I can go hog wild and buy milk *and* coffee!

Monday. Tuesday. Wednesday. No checks. Thursday. Still no checks. I resolve not to panic. Any minute now, all my money will come, and everything will be fine. Why, I'll even be able to buy bread, not just milk and coffee! I will also be able to start digging into that mountain of looming bills. There's no reason to worry.

The following day is January 11, and I check the mail again. No check from my agency. I finally panic and contact them. They didn't realize they had forgotten to tell me that there'd been a clerical error which had prevented them from mailing the check as planned. Sorry!

No check for my column, either. The treasurer's computer has had some sort of massive meltdown, and checks will be late this month.

There *is* a check from my old reliable friends at Tekno Books, Martin H. Greenberg's company, the people for whom I have written so many short stories. Tekno are the only people I've ever written for who always pay me promptly. I knew they would come through! But...

The check is made out to another writer.

Tekno, for the first time in all the years I've been working with them, have sent me the wrong check. I phone them, try-ing to keep my voice calm. They apologize, ask me to send the check back, and promise to hunt down *my* check and send it as soon as possible.

I was obviously a really bad person in a previous life. (Though I suppose some people would assert that I've just been a bad one in *this* life.)

I mean...Good God! Three checks due, none arrived. What are the odds?

I have hysterics. I fling myself into walls. I cry and rage and carry on. I CAN'T TAKE THIS ANYMORE! I can't live like this anymore!!! Who could? I'm done! Through! Finished! I don't want to write anymore! I don't want to belong to this crazy, awful, mixed-up, slobbering excuse of a profession anymore! I should have done anything else with my life except *this*! I QUIT!!!

Like generations of writers before me, I finally lose my mind.

Writer Valerie Taylor shows up at my place an hour later

to collect a table that I borrowed from her for my Christmas party. Crazy and unkempt, I ask her to feed me. She is a soft-hearted person and takes me to lunch, pouring glasses of wine down my throat until I finally calm down enough to stop making wild-eyed death-threats.

The following week, all of my checks come. I enter into an orgy of paying bills and buying groceries. But my nerves are so frayed that surely only another trip to France will cure me.

Myriam, please book me a flight on the next plane out of this popsicle stand.

Back in the Day

My friend Sheila lives in a beautifully renovated, three-floor, Victorian townhouse in Chelsea, an upscale neighborhood of London. When the French science fiction/fantasy concom (conference committee) flew me over to Europe for "Utopia," to eat all their food, drink all their wine, and do virtually nothing in return, I had the airplane drop me off in London first, where I stayed with Sheila for a while.

I lived in London for three years in the mid-1980s, and it remains one of my favorite cities in the world. And since I have friends located all over the country, I really enjoy visiting the U.K. when I get the chance. Sheila, however, is not actually a friend from my London days. She's an American, like me. We met when we were both twenty-one, broke, and living in New York City.

Back then, Sheila and I both worked for a little import-export company peopled by a bizarre cast of characters. Our chain-smoking foreign boss was volatile and colorful. I always thought his well-dressed Egyptian partner seemed more like a high-level assassin than a businessman. I was hired to assist a jet-setting, multi-lingual

Englishman who went to the Italian Alps and the Egyptian pyramids on his weekends—from New York. Sheila was the assistant of a soft-spoken guy who had fled Cuba when the Russians got interested in taking him to Moscow to study at some sort of academy for making bigger and better nuclear weapons during the Cold War. Our receptionist was a refugee from El Salvador, born to an illiterate housemaid and the upper-class playboy who'd had his way with her. The company's beautiful French-Japanese comptroller had an assistant who was an Afghan aristocrat in exile. The incredibly well-dressed Chinese woman who shared my alcove fought loudly on the phone almost every day with her American husband. In the exotic atmosphere of this intercultural company, Sheila and I, a couple of middle-class Midwestern kids fresh out of college, became friends and stuck together.

Sheila and her roommate lived in a one-bedroom, fifth-floor walk-up that had a bathtub in the kitchen. I had a variety of roommates and a variety of apartments—culminating in a sixth-floor walk-up (yes: six floors, no elevator) where the hot water regularly ran out. I subletted the place from a stage manager, and I shared it with a model who was seldom there. Since rent and other expenses in New York were so high, Sheila and I both had second jobs in restaurants on the weekends; I worked in a place with two enormous scowling bouncers (one of whom was a preschool teacher by day).

Within a year, I abandoned New York for Europe. Later, of course, I eventually returned to Ohio and became a novelist. Sheila eventually left the import-export firm for a better job, then later left New York to get her MBA at Georgetown University (my alma mater, where I studied languages and linguistics—thereby enabling me to make friends in bars all over the world).

Now, years later, Sheila has a career in finance. I don't know what she does exactly (even though she's explained it to me several times), but I assume she must be pretty good at it, since she's been promoted to posts in Belgium, Ireland, and England, she lives in an enormous flat in a fashionable borough, and she drives a car so nice you could eat off it.

Now, whenever Sheila and I get together, we marvel all over again at the joy of no longer climbing six flights of stairs at the end of each day, no longer showering in the kitchen, and no longer waiting tables on the weekends. Yes, getting older has its compensations. In the spring of 1984, I was a penniless secretary/waitress with incredibly tired legs. Last autumn, I was an award-winning professional writer lolling around Sheila's luxurious London flat while a French convention picked up the tab for my trans-Atlantic trip. Who says my life ain't working out?

Anyhow, I had a wonderful time in London. It was my first visit there in six years. I spent time with Sheila, reacquainted myself with the city of my delightfully misspent youth, caught up with old friends and their families, attended world-class art exhibitions, saw first-rate theatrical performances, and haunted the halls of some of the most extraordinary museums on the planet. I had such fun that I decided I mustn't let nearly so much time pass before I visited again. Sheila generously assured me that I am welcome to stay with her anytime the guest room is empty.

So when she subsequently e-mailed me to say she was being transferred Stateside, I decided to try to squeeze in another visit to her before she left London. After all, I had recently sold two books, and I could afford the trip, thanks to the nice raise my agent had negotiated for me. A springtime visit to London seemed like the perfect way to celebrate!

Within twenty-four hours, though, I was forced to abandon

these plans, go on a diet of bread and water, and contemplate taking up highway robbery as a secondary profession.

I'm sure you'll understand the evil implications when I say: I received my tax bill.

✳

In *Thus Was Adonis Murdered*, a British mystery novel by the late Sarah Caudwell, one of the characters—a tax attorney, like Caudwell herself—finds herself stuck in a vicious cycle. Each year, she's hit with such a heavy tax bill that she must work longer hours and earn more money in order to pay it. The resultant increase in her income ensures that the following year's tax bill is even bigger, thereby requiring her to further increase her income in order to pay it, which thus results in the following year's tax bill being even bigger due to the increase in her earnings, and so on and so forth.

Where will it all end? the desperate character wonders.

I, too, will need to make more money now in order to cover the unforeseen size of this year's tax bill. That means that I, too, will find next year's tax bill even bigger than this year's, and will have to earn even more next year to pay it. And so on and so forth.

Like the character in Caudwell's novel, I now find myself thinking it was probably a mistake ever to begin paying taxes in the first place. It has led to the IRS taking shameless advantage of me ever since.

✳

My friend Valerie Taylor comes over again, and she finds me moping about my tax bill, which I've received that morning. I'm so traumatized by the experience that it will probably be weeks before I can bring myself to open the mailbox again. I advise Val to enjoy the food on my table while it lasts, since I obviously won't be buying any more this year.

She comes up with a whimsical proposal for a taxation scheme whereby artists, writers, and musicians whose annual income is below a certain level would not be required to pay income tax. This system, she explains, would be an equitable exchange for choosing to subsist below a certain income level in favor of pursuing one's art.

Having listened to her attempt to cheer me up with such lighthearted distraction, I now open a bottle and pour myself a very big glass of wine.

The scheme would be redundant, anyhow. Statistically speaking, I remind Val, the average writer in this country doesn't earn enough to be taxed on his writing income. Well, not taxed seriously. Not taxed the way *I* am being taxed, for example. Not taxed to the extent that he may have to go get a part-time job to pay the tax bill on his full-time writing income. Not taxed to the extent that he has to abandon plans to upgrade the computer equipment he uses in his writing career. Not taxed to the extent that he wonders if he'll have to sell an additional book this year to make up for the mistake of having sold one last year, and then sell two additional books next year to make up for the mistake of having sold an additional one this year. Not taxed to the extent that his vacation plans were smothered at birth!

Having listened to me, Val pours herself a very big glass of wine.

That night, CNN does a feature on a theatrical production I dearly want to see.

It's showing in London.

❋

In fact, it was theatre which took me to London in the first place. Back in the day, I thought I wanted to be an actress. So I auditioned and got accepted to a post-graduate course at a London drama school and thereby wound up moving overseas. I chose to study in England because I had always admired British actors so much—particularly upon seeing them on-stage when I was living in New York. (We used to line up at a half-price ticket booth after work to get cheap same-day seats.)

Well, acting's an even harder life than writing, and I'm not the only one of my fellow students from the academy to wind up in another profession. Several of them did become successful working actors, but others, like me, found their true calling elsewhere. Despite my love-hate relationship with writing, after I sold a book I never once looked back at the acting dreams I'd abandoned. I am so suited to this work, and so unsuited to the work I once thought I wanted to do. I found my true profession early in life, and even I know enough to be grateful for that.

Nonetheless, it's fair to say that studying acting taught me most of what I know about characterization and dialogue as a writer. There are other things—such as conflict, structure, and pace—which I knew nothing about when I sold my first book and had to study hard to learn on the job, so to speak. But the intense focus that my drama training gave to character development, intention, motivation, subtext, backstory, action, reaction, and interaction, and to all the different ways of delivering dialogue and the different meanings it could convey—whether post-modern surrealism, or classic verse, or naturalism—taught me a great deal that I was able to translate into my work as a writer. Acting taught me to get inside the skin, minds, and hearts of a broad variety of characters—which is, of course, what a good writer has to learn to do.

I've never gotten inside the skin, mind, and heart of an IRS agent, though. Even in my art, there are limits past which I will not go.

✳

My tax bill this year is, as always, tucked inside the dull, plain, conservative blue folder in which my accountant delivers the bad news every year. "Dull, plain, and conservative" is, I have always been told, more or less what one wants in an accountant, so I find the color of the envelope reassuring, even though its presence on my desk is reminiscent of a sleeping viper.

I looked at it once when it arrived. Immediately felt hot, faint, and queasy. Fell into a depression. Nearly succumbed to tears. Drank a little too much wine with lunch. Since then, I've been doing things like turning off all the lights, walking instead of using gas by taking the car, and rinsing resealable plastic bags for reuse instead of throwing them away as if I could afford such careless waste.

At some point, of course, I will have to pull out the envelope, thoroughly read my tax returns, sign them...and then write a check to the IRS.

For now, though, the blue folder sits on my desk, silently condemning. A mute reminder of all the money which is suddenly no longer mine. Wordlessly goading me with the knowledge that the better my career gets and the more I earn...the more the IRS will make me suffer for it.

Where will it all end? the desperate novelist wonders.

The Wages of Obsession

I'm busy saving the world when the phone rings, so I ignore it. It keeps ringing; so, naturally, I turn off the ringer.

Ambitious sorcerers, conflict-haunted warriors, thirsty goddesses, and the armies of empires do not stop for a phone call, so neither can I.

A couple of days later, I notice that no one has phoned me in days, and I begin to wonder why. When the silence continues, I start to feel petulant and neglected.

As two characters exchange insults in my work-in-progress, I write one of them saying to the other, "No one likes you. No one has ever liked you."

The silence persists, and I wonder if I've alienated everyone who knows me because I haven't emerged from my hole for a while. Maybe they've forgotten me entirely?

Finally, because I (let's keep in mind) have the razor-sharp perception needed to save the world, I realize that I forgot to turn the ringer back on after the last time I turned it off.

This happens a lot, actually.

Satisfied at having solved the mystery, I return to work.

An unforeseen event erupts in the story, surprising me. I love when this happens! If the story surprises *me*, then I know it'll surprise the reader. If *I* didn't see something coming, then I'm not in danger of telegraphing it to the reader. If I'm not sure where this is going, then even after I've figured it out, I know the reader won't be sure where this is going—and will therefore, I hope, feel compelled to stay up late, turning pages.

When unplanned developments erupt, unfold, and slide into the story while I'm writing, I know it means this bird is taking flight. It wants to spread its wings, and all I have to do is stick with it, serve it, feed it...and then clean up all its messes. That is to say, this eruption (like so many of them) creates more work: I'll have to go back through the preceding chapters to plant the necessary foreshadowing for this new development.

The phone rings. (See? That's what happens when you turn it back on. Simple cause and effect.)

Since planting foreshadowing is tedious work that makes my head hurt, I feel ready to take a break, so I reach for the receiver.

"Hello?"

"Did I wake you?" my friend Karen asks. "You sound like you've been asleep."

"Huh? No. I'm working."

"Where have you been? I've been trying to reach you for days!"

"Huh?" Ah-hah! I think I know an ideal spot for the foreshadowing. But...it means I'll need to shift one event in that spot to another scene, or the foreshadowing material will seem out of place.

"Did you turn off the phone?" Karen asks. "Is that why you haven't been answering it?"

"Huh?" Now, if I shift *that* event to...No, that won't work. Hmmm...Do I really need the segment that needs shifting? Could I just eject it from the book altogether? Oops, no, it has to be there or some motivation loses strength. But could the event occur in another scene, in another character's point of view?

"Laura, are you listening to me?"

"Huh?"

✳

I grew up in a writer's house. So I vowed that I was *never* going to be like that.

I remember my father, a science fiction writer, staring off into space over his dinner plate on many occasions during my childhood. Sometimes his lips would move without any sound coming out. Sometimes he'd suddenly cry, "Ah-hah!" or "Got it!" for no apparent reason, then trot off to his typewriter.

No sir, not me, I was never going to be like *that*.

✳

"Where are you?" Valerie Taylor says at the other end of my phone one day.

"Huh?" I'm starting to suspect I've staged this love scene too soon. It lacks sufficient power if it comes this early.

Val reminds me that I was supposed to pick her up to go to a mutual friend's house today.

I explain she's wrong, because—I check my calendar to be sure—that's not until Sunday. I know this for a fact. I am in complete control of my life.

"Today *is* Sunday, Laura."

Oops.

I wonder what scene I can swap with the love scene. And where, then, would the love scene need to go? Oh, hell, I should probably just scrap the love scene, because it'll be different from what I've written now, anyhow, if it comes later.

"Did I wake you?" Val asks.

✳

I pull an all-nighter when the dam finally bursts on what has been a particularly stubborn section of a manuscript. Then, pleased with what I've finally accomplished after a long struggle with this work, I take a sleep-inducing migraine-killer for my skull-splitting headache and crawl into bed at dawn wearing a barely-dirty T-shirt that I find lying atop a pile of laundry which comprises every item of clothing I own.

Later that morning, I hear some water hitting my open bedroom window. How bizarre. I pull a pillow over my head and hope the water will just go away. The phone rings; I'm too tired to get up to turn off the ringer, so I just ignore it. A little while later, through my pillow, I hear pounding on my front door. Exhausted and exasperated, I drag the quilt up over my pillow-covered head. After a long night of pulling this damn book back together at last, I feel as if I've been lobotomized. If the world doesn't let me get some damn *sleep* now, I will not be responsible for the consequences!

Through the weight of all the goose-down hiding me from the world, I hear a strange sound in my bedroom. Some flicker of awareness kicks in, making me realize that unexplained noises in my own bedroom could be worth investigating. I push aside muffling pillows and quilt, sit up—and come face-to-face with my *stunned* landlord, who's trying to close my open windows so workmen can continue power-washing the building.

I barely register that I am not, after all, in danger, then I collapse into unconsciousness while this man I scarcely know is still in my bedroom.

❋

One time, when I was a kid, another science fiction writer came to our house for dinner.

Five days later, she and her husband were still there.

She and my father sat at opposite ends of the dining room table each day and night, typing furiously, while her husband paced behind her and read the pages coming off her hot typewriter.

They only left when our water well finally exploded—but that's another story entirely.

Writers, I learned when I was young, don't have a normal sense of time. Their internal clocks work in a mysterious warp of reality which can turn day into night, hours into minutes, and dinner into a five-day visit.

I, however, was going to grow up to be like normal people.

❋

Early one evening, I save the day's work to my zip disk, turn off the computer, realize I won't have time for a shower, and do what I can with my appearance.

I leave the house...only to return three minutes later when I realize I've forgotten the wine I bought for my hosts.

I leave the house again...only to return when I realize I

haven't been to my friends' house in so long that I need to get driving directions on Yahoo.

I make it all the way to the end of the street this time...then have to turn back to the neighborhood gas station when I realize I don't have enough in the tank to make it out to the suburbs.

I finally get to the suburbs and discover...I left my Yahoo driving directions back in my office.

This is my life.

I vaguely remember where my friends live and just hunt until I find the house. I arrive only a few minutes late despite my various setbacks.

My hostess starts laughing when she greets me. "You're here on the wrong day, Laura."

Impossible!

"No way," I say. "This is Friday. I double-checked the calendar only this morning. Today is Friday!"

"You're right," she says, "today is Friday. But I told you dinner is for Saturday."

This is my life every damn day.

The parents of a close friend, my hosts have known me most of my life, so they're not as surprised by my unexpected arrival as casual acquaintances might be. Since I've driven all this way, they make a three-way division of their casual dinner for two and feed me. In exchange, I endure predictable ribbing at the dinner party they have the following evening while their daughter, my longtime friend, is in town for the night.

"I've been working hard lately," I say in my defense.

✳

One day I decide I hate my protagonist's name.

I keep changing it, and five minutes after I think I've finally found the right name...I hate it again. I've been doing this since yesterday. I'm still pouring over baby books, phone directories, and arcane lists when the phone rings.

"Did I wake you?" my friend Jerry Spradlin asks me.

"No." Why does everyone always ask me that? "I'm working."

"Oh. You sound like you've been sleeping."

"What do you want?"

Jerry has been trying to reach me for a while and wonders if something was wrong with my phone.

"What do you want?" I repeat.

Jerry has been a mine of research information for me over the years. He studies exotic, highly practical, and lethal martial arts. If my fantasy characters know how to kill, wound, maim, attack, and survive convincingly, much of that is due to what I've learned from Jerry. If my contemporary fiction characters know anything about guns, it's because Jerry has taken me to a shooting range.

Now Jerry's calling to discuss a scene in my new work-in-progress. I described the scene to him the other day and asked him for suggestions, from a combat standpoint, for the surprise conclusion the scene needs. The idea he came up with not only works with the plot, but is also great in terms of the book's tone.

So I was satisfied; but he, he now tells me, has been thinking about it since then. He's got more ideas for it.

It's contagious, this obsession.

✳

As I type these words, almost every item of clothing I own is in a mountain of laundry in the living room. I'll have to do at least one load today, or else go buy more underpants.

Carry-out pizza boxes are stacked in the kitchen, and the garbage can is an archaeological treasure trove of my nutritional fare when on a very tight deadline, as I have been for the past two weeks: Empty cookie cartons, empty cheese cracker cartons, empty antacid cartons, empty coffee cans.

I suspect I am getting too old to live this way.

More likely, I am getting too old to choose any other life.

"Writing is an obsession and a way of life," I've heard novelist Mary Jo Putney say.

As I look back at the sensible child I once was, though, I am more inclined to quote Karen Blixen, a writer who was probably quoting yet another writer, when she said, "The earth was made round so that we could not see too far down the road."

Orphans of the Storm

O nce upon a time (come on, who doesn't love a story that begins that way?), I sold my first book, a romance novel, to Silhouette Books, a division of Harlequin Enterprises (a.k.a. The Evil Empire).

As first sales go, it was a fairly painless process. Several months after I sent them my manuscript, I received an encouraging letter from an editorial assistant saying she liked my book and was passing it higher up the food chain. A few months after that, I received another letter from her saying that the book was getting favorable readings, but acquiring a new author was a lengthy process at Silhouette, one which required patience and time. Then, about eleven months after I'd mailed in the manuscript, I received a FedEx letter from an editor at Silhouette; they'd been trying to reach me for several days, but there was no answer at the phone number I'd given them, and so they wanted me to call them.

(This was back in the spring of 1988. I didn't have a computer, I had never heard of e-mail, and I didn't own an answering machine.)

So I phoned them. The editor who'd signed the letter answered the phone, gushed nicely about my writing, and made me an offer for the book—an offer that was roughly the advance sum which, based on my research, I expected from them. The editor (whose name I've long since forgotten) praised my talent and said she would like to see everything else I had written. She explained that she'd be interested in buying as many as four books a year from me if I could write fast enough.

I was, needless to say, thrilled!

The editor's revision requests on that first book were neither arduous nor unreasonable. I completed them easily, turned in the final manuscript, and got paid. And, as requested, I sent her the rest of my work: two more complete manuscripts, and one partial.

The next time I heard from my editor was when I received a letter from her announcing she was leaving Silhouette and, indeed, leaving the publishing industry entirely (which is why I don't even remember her name anymore). Her last day in the office, to answer questions or deal with her writers, was the day the letter was mailed and (obviously) several days before I received it. Her letter assured me I would soon be assigned to a new editor. She didn't make any mention of the manuscripts that I had sent her at her request.

When I finally received another letter informing me who my new editor was, I phoned her so that we could get acquainted, talk about the book that I had in production there, and talk about the manuscripts which were now presumably sitting on her desk.

I only remember her first name, and only because it was so comically unsuited to her personality: Joy. She was a rather listless, sour person who told me that I'd been shoveled onto her already too-heavy workload along with a bunch of other writers whom, like me, she really didn't want or have time for.

I asked when my first novel was scheduled for release. Joy didn't know and was "too busy" to find out.

I asked about the three manuscripts which I had submitted at my previous editor's request. Joy didn't know and was too busy to find out. I reminded her of my option clause; Silhouette had sixty days, from submission, to give me an answer on those manuscripts. She coldly informed me she had no idea when she'd have time to read them.

A couple of months passed with no contact from Joy. So I phoned her. She never phoned back. I phoned her again. She still didn't phone back. I phoned yet again—and caught her at her desk this time. She hadn't looked at my manuscripts, had no idea where they were, was too busy to look for them, and didn't really have time to waste talking to me. I reminded her that the option period had now expired, so an answer would be appropriate. She responded with irritable indifference and ended the conversation.

I had been (perhaps you've heard the term before) *orphaned*.

This is one of the many pitfalls of publishing that you don't really think about (and perhaps don't even hear about) when you're trying to break into the business. While it doesn't happen often, it's nonetheless a typical enough experience that a writer should be aware of the possibility.

Being "orphaned" usually means that your editor leaves the publishing house, for one reason or another, and the editor who gets you in her place doesn't particularly want you or care about your career. She didn't discover you, didn't acquire you—she's merely *inherited* you, and she clearly wishes she hadn't.

Some writers wind up leaving publishing houses (involuntarily) after being orphaned; because it's not just the publisher who buys and believes in your work—it is very specifically and importantly the *editor*. Without an editor interested in your work and championing you within the house, you probably have no real future there.

Now, let's clarify: Being orphaned does not *necessarily* lead to problems. There are numerous instances where your new editor is just as enthused about your writing as your old one was, perhaps even more so. There are many instances where you are just as compatible with your new editor as you were with her predecessor, perhaps even more so. There are editors who inherit you and automatically call you up to tell you how excited they are about working with you hereafter. There are editors who, before making that call, spend all weekend reading everything you've published with their house so they can chat intelligently with you about your work. So let's not panic. Being orphaned is not always a disaster. It's not even always an awkward or difficult thing.

In my case, however, it was a genuine career crisis. I knew no one at Silhouette Books, and none of them knew me. I had no agent and no one to advocate for me. I was a brand new writer with one modest sale under my belt. It's very common for writers to disappear after just one or two sales, so no one at Silhouette would have ever wondered why I had never survived beyond my first book with them. I was powerless and friendless, and I had been inherited by an editor who very clearly just wanted to get *rid* of me. An editor who wanted me to disappear, because I represented nothing to her except extra work that she didn't want. An editor who, just by stalling me, rejecting me, and dodging my calls, had the ability to *make* me disappear.

This went on for five months. The closest Joy ever got to

reading my work was to farm out one of my manuscripts to a free-lance reader who, she then told me, gave it an "unfavorable report." Joy explained to me that, based on that reaction, she herself didn't expect to like any of my work, and she doubted that I would make another sale to Silhouette.

Wow, can't get much clearer than that, can she?

I panicked. I knew that in order to save my fledgling career, I had to do something to get past this (I use the word loosely) editor. She was a serious impediment to my professional survival. So I did something I almost *never* do: I sought the advice of my father, science fiction writer Mike Resnick.

At his suggestion, I wrote a carefully worded letter to Joy's boss. I praised Joy effusively…and remarked on how terrible I felt about the way she was so overworked. I commented on her tremendous work ethic and personal charm…and mourned that she was so busy, she'd gone five months without having a chance to read any of my optioned manuscripts. I expressed tremendous admiration for Joy…while reflecting that it just seemed unfair that she was afflicted with so many writers she didn't even have time to return my phone calls. And I nobly volunteered to be assigned to another editor—someone who, while perhaps lacking Joy's warmth, brilliance, and efficiency, might actually have a chance to read my submissions.

In other words, I asked for a new editor and explained my reasons, while being careful not to openly criticize the one I was with. I also copied the letter to Joy herself, so that I wouldn't appear to be going behind her back or trying to stir up trouble.

It worked. Joy's boss phoned me personally for a long, friendly chat. She never criticized Joy in our conversation, but she clearly understood that it was a bad situation and I needed to be moved. Within a week or two, I was reassigned to another editor—one who spent the weekend reading the book I had under contract there *and* all of my new submissions, then phoned me, made me an offer, talked about how enthused she was about working with me hereafter, and did all the other things that a good editor does when she inherits a writer. She and I worked together for several years at Silhouette, and we have remained friendly ever since those days. So the story has a happy ending.

So, when your editorial relationship isn't working out, you can ask for a new editor. A smart publisher knows that editors and writers work better when they're teamed with the right individuals. (Unfortunately, not all publishers are smart; but if you don't ask, you'll never know.)

However, if you're going to do this, your editorial problems need to be real problems, not just a case of an editor who didn't buy a book you wanted to sell her, or whose personality you're not that crazy about. Also, remember that although most publishing houses will humor this request once, they'll rarely do it twice; if you have problems with your subsequent editor there, then *you* are likely to be regarded as the problem. So before asking for a new editor, make sure that you're positive that *any* change would be an improvement. (In my situation with Joy, I was *quite* positive.)

Asking for a new editor, while well within your rights as a writer, is a delicate political move. You may have many good reasons to hate the editor, but she is an employee (possibly even a favored and longtime one) of the house. It's usually best to have your agent deal with this. If you don't have an agent, as I didn't, then it's best to be as tactful and non-accusatory as possible, while nonetheless making your needs known to your editor's superior.

As for Joy...she left publishing forever only a few weeks after I got reassigned, so you're in no danger of running into her. (A lot of editors you'll meet along the way leave publishing forever. Really. It's not just the ones who work with *me*.)

And remember the editorial assistant who kept sending me nice encouraging letters before my first sale? She later became my editor for a couple of years. She eventually left the business, but we've remained friends all these years. (And just to clarify: She did not leave the business because of *me*, okay?)

In Praise of Old Friends

"It is a truth universally acknowledged that a single man in possession of a good fortune must be in want of a wife."

Is there anyone among us who doesn't recognize the opening line of Jane Austen's most celebrated novel?

Well, who knows? Perhaps there is. No shame in that. Books are as individual as people, and our tastes in them vary just as much as we ourselves do. Maybe you don't recognize the opening line of *Pride and Prejudice*, but you could recite the entire first paragraph of *From Here to Eternity* or *The Joy Luck Club* or the latest Dan Brown novel. I know people who've never read Austen, just as I know people who are astonished that I've never read Kurt Vonnegut. I know people who look at me cross-eyed after I loan them one of my favorite novels, Edward Whittemore's *Sinai Tapestry*, just as I gaped open-mouthed at a friend who told me *The Bridges of Madison County* was the best book she'd ever read.

As Andre Maurois said, "In literature, as in love, we are astonished at what is chosen by others."

The most astonishing thing to me, though, is someone who chooses nothing at all. Okay, sure, if you're a starving war captive in the Sudan, you may not even know how to read, and the lack of books is probably nowhere among your one hundred most pressing problems. But who can understand the people here, among us, in our own culture, on our own doorstep, who don't read? Who can understand the people who don't love books?

I sure can't. I have a lifelong addiction to taking trips which are possible only in my imagination, and I don't want to be cured. My addiction is fostered, nurtured, cultivated, and fed by the characters I've met and come to love (or hate) on the printed page; the tragedies and comedies in which I have participated through the act of reading; the worlds and lives and times I have experienced through the gift of a writer's imagination reaching out to stir mine.

So when Jane Austen's charming, shrewd, cultivated voice reaches out to me across the span of two centuries, how could I refuse the invitation to join in the loves, lives, conflicts, and schemes of her delightful characters in the vivid world she presents to me?

My volume of Austen's collected works used to belong to my mother. The pages are yellowing, the spine is very bent, I don't recall it ever having had a dust jacket, and, at one time, I badly smeared the front endpaper in an attempt to mark it with my name; and I know you'll understand when I say that it's precious to me, just as it is. My copy of *Little Women* is in even worse shape. It's a post-WWII Grosset & Dunlap edition with color as well as black-and-white illustrations. It was also my mother's, though it was my grandmother who gave it to me. The pages are dog-eared, some of them torn, and there's a faint musty smell when I open it—which I seldom do, because the spine is unraveling. But I don't want a new copy, and I don't need to open it to remember the details which most captivated me about the lives of the March girls in mid-nineteenth century America.

My copy of W. Somerset Maugham's *The Razor's Edge*, printed during WWII, is in pretty good shape. I have no memory of where I got it, though a stranger's name is on the front endpaper, mostly concealed by the dustjacket, and a pencil notation indicates that I must have picked it up for two dollars somewhere, long ago. More than twenty years ago, I suppose, since I was a teenager the first time I read it. I've read it three more times since then, following Maugham's friends to Europe and Asia, voyaging in an exotic long-ago world of well-turned phrases, and sharing in Larry's spiritual quest during the years between the wars. A close friend of mine sometimes identifies a whirlpool of emotional denial and self-absorption encountered in real life through a simple code phrase, derived from reading that novel, when she says to me, "Isabel doesn't get it."

Three, four, five times isn't unusual for me to read a favorite book. I'm blessed with a terrible memory, so I can re-read my favorites often, remembering very little about them except that I know for a fact I'll really enjoy them, whereas new reads are more of a crap-shoot. Nonetheless, a healthy balance between old and new is essential, because it is in new reads that we find the works which add to our supply of cherished old friends, our treasure trove of best-beloved books that we dust, tend, mend, alphabetize, re-read, and hoard as if they were made of gold rather than pulp.

Had I not experimented with new reads in recent years, I wouldn't have discovered Loretta Chase, Iain Pears, Tanya

Huff, Sparkle Hayter, and numerous other writers whose books I now tend and dust and make space for in an ever-more crowded shelving system. When Mary Jo Putney's Reggie Davenport explains in *The Rake* that he can't just rest on his laurels, because wickedness requires constant effort, I knew I had found a new favorite. When I deserted real life for three straight days because I hadn't yet reached a place in Katherine Neville's *The Eight* where I could bear to put the book down, I had found a new favorite. When non-fiction writer Diane Ackerman mesmerized me with an entire chapter on the sense of *smell*, in her *A Natural History of the Senses*, I found a new favorite.

But the old friends, the books I've been reading and re-reading for years...those are special in the way that treasured personal mementos, shared recollections, and old photo albums are special. Those novels are as much as part of my past as the paperweight next to me that belonged to my grandfather, the photo on my wall of a friend who died young, the scar on my knee from summer camp in 1970, or the shoe-shaped brush I bought in Holland after a group of Dutch strangers all pooled their spare cash to donate to me when my wallet was stolen. My life would be barren without these memories; and I don't want to imagine it without these books, either.

There are certain Barbara Michaels and Elizabeth Peters novels I've read half a dozen times apiece. Her real name, by the way, is Barbara Mertz, and she is, among other things, an Egyptologist holding a Ph.D. from the University of Chicago (where, incidentally, a veritable slew of my relatives went, too). She's lived in Maryland for years, and has set a number of her wonderful novels in that area. When I went east to Georgetown University as a college kid, I initially felt homesick and out of place in Washington, D.C. To keep myself from panicking, I re-read *Ammie, Come Home*, which took place in the very neighborhood where I was living, as well as other novels of Barbara's set in the region: *Witch, The Prince of Darkness, The Walker in the Shadows, Patriot's Dream, House of Many Shadows...* Toward the end of my senior year, a newsletter for Barbara's readers announced a contest, which I entered and won by writing a story outline which she liked. My prize was the original cover painting of one of my favorite Michaels novels, *The Sea King's Daughter*; but Barbara had to hold onto it for me because I left the country right after college and went for a long time without a fixed address. We thereby became correspondents. Ever since those days, I still get uncharacteristically gushy about the fact that one of my all-time favorite novelists refers to *me* as a friend. (You may touch my hem.) I couldn't even count how many times I've read *The Dark on the Other Side*, which delights and terrifies me every single time I read it. Her *Wait for What Will Come* is the book I read whenever I'm sick, as the characters, setting, and story enchant and comfort me when I'm feeling my worst. (I'm so predictable that, one time, novelist Kathy Chwedyk called here, discovered I had the flu, and automatically assumed—correctly—that I was therefore re-reading that book, as well as another great Michaels favorite, her spine-tingling *The Crying Child*.)

It was through Barbara Mertz that I once briefly met Sarah Caudwell. I decided that anyone so funny might well be worth reading, and I picked up her first three books. Since then, I've read them all almost every single year, always delighted anew by the witty, elegant world I enter when I open a Caudwell novel. I want to hang out and pal around with these funny, urbane, clever people in their thoroughly enchant-ing settings; and, by reading these books, I get to do so.

Caudwell's final novel, *The Sibyl in Her Grave*, was released posthumously, the author having died of cancer several months earlier. At the risk of sounding insensitive, if she weren't already dead, I would kill her for writing only four books before she left this world. I want twenty. I want forty. I want *more*.

Somebody else who left me wanting more is John Bellairs, a children's writer who wrote just one adult novel (though it's a great read for kids, too) in his life. It happens to be my all-time favorite fantasy novel, *The Face in the Frost*. This perfect gem is both charming and terrifying, whimsical and dark, funny and tense. I've looked for twenty years to find another novel to give me the same feeling of fantastical enchantment which this one does, because one is not enough.

Along with Bellairs, another science fiction/fantasy writer I never tire of re-reading is C.L. Moore, a woman writing in this male-dominated genre back in the 1930s. Although she also wrote novels, my great passion is for her series of fantasy short stories centered around the medieval adventuress Jirel of Joiry, as well as for her science fictional short story series about a space adventurer named Northwest Smith. I have all these stories in two illustrated specialty-press anthologies. Moore's ability to captivate me transcends reality in a tangible way, since her science fiction stories postulated a solar system which we now know to be wholly inaccurate. In the author's vision, our neighboring planets are all populated with native races and cultures; and when Moore writes, I believe that Venusians and Martians, their cities and communities, are really *there*, despite what NASA space probes show us.

Every beloved novel (*Trade Wind*, *A River Sutra*, *Cry*

the Beloved Country, *Seize the Fire*, *Lincoln's Dreams*, *Catch-22*, etc., etc.) in my bookcases, every treasured writer (Georgette Heyer, Mary Stewart, Oscar Wilde, etc., etc.) whom I re-read is a refuge, a resource, a wellspring. Every book I re-open is a homecoming. Every story I return to is a friend embracing me.

I can never understand the people who choose to turn their backs on all of this. My love of all of this was so over-whelming it turned me into a storyteller—as if I could ever give back what all these writers have given to me. I can only be passionate, positive, grateful, and endlessly enthusiastic about all the fabulous writers and all the wonderful books—too many to name here—which have made my life, pretty rich and varied in its own right, so much more than it would have been without them.

Sometimes it's good to take a moment and offer them the praise they deserve.

Going Public

It's January in Detroit. Saturday afternoon. I'm visiting friends, and, as long as I'm here anyhow, I've arranged a signing at a local new-and-used bookstore that has been recommended as a romance-friendly place.

(This is, you will gather, a Saturday afternoon in my innocent youth, back when I was romance writer Laura Leone—an era of my life which science fiction/fantasy people, for reasons which elude me, sometimes treat as a dark secret, or else as so irrelevant that they refer to me as a "new" writer even though I've been in the business for years. So jumping genres and changing names is one way to keep the damask bloom on your fragrant cheek, I suppose. But I digress.)

Where was I?

Oh, yes. In Detroit. In a January past. With a new romance novel on the stands, and a signing scheduled at a bookstore not far from the home of my tolerant friends Cindy and Bob Person—whose illusions about the glamorous life of a novelist were shattered long ago due to knowing me.

The bookstore—in contrast to Cindy and Bob's warm, dry, well-lit house—is damp and chilly and dark. The few items of my wardrobe that are suitable for public appearances weren't made for Michigan winters, and I sit shivering by the radiator—which is the coldest thing in the store.

Within minutes of my arrival, the light snowfall outside turns into a heavy snowstorm. In my hometown of Cincinnati, we're notorious for abandoning our cars, shutting down our schools, and emptying our grocery stores of bread, milk, and beer at the first sign of snow. (We also did this throughout the week of race riots there in the Spring of 2001. If CNN announced that an atomic bomb was about to land on our city, Cincinnatians would rush out to the store for more bread, milk, and beer. It's our way.) However, I expected the hardy citizens of Michigan to be made of sterner stuff. I was wrong. Even in Michigan, people don't go shopping in a snowstorm.

So the store is completely deserted for the first ninety minutes of my two-hour booksigning.

In the absence of anything else to do, the bookseller tries chatting with me as I huddle and shiver. The essence of her conversation is that *last* week's signing here went so well by comparison. The author on that auspicious day was Shelly Thacker, who is so *charming* and so *pretty*, and who has such a wonderful personality. Shelly Thacker is also so *considerate*, because *she* brought homemade cookies with her. And she's so popular and such a wonderful writer that there were lines around the block when she was signing here!

Are you out there Shelly Thacker? Don't take this the wrong way, but the next time we meet, I will be forced to kill you. I'm sure you understand.

Finally, after the longest ninety minutes of my luckless

life, the snowfall thins out to flurries. And before you know it—hurrah!—a customer enters the store. A regular, obviously, since she and the bookseller know each other. The bookseller introduces me and points out the piles of my new book which are sitting on the table in front of me. The customer brusquely rejects the suggestion that she might be interested in my book, and she disappears into the bowels of the store. She emerges from the stacks ten minutes later with a few books...including a second-hand copy of one of my previous titles.

As she's paying for it at the cash register, the bookseller suggests to her that I'd be happy to sign it for her. As I sit grinding my teeth in mute protest, the customer looks me over assessingly from head-to-toe, and then says, "No, I'm sure I'll be bringing it back next week."

And people wonder why I long ago gave up arranging signings for my books. (Cindy and Bob do not wonder, of course, because they had to spend the rest of that Saturday listening to me gripe.)

Not that I'm the only writer whose signing ever went belly-up because of bad weather. Bestselling romance novelist Jill Marie Landis recalls being in a car with a driver on her way to do a signing at a Barnes and Noble in Oklahoma City once: "It starts pouring. Lightning. Thunder. Tornado warnings out. We are headed for a really huge black cloud. We get to the bookstore. The driver gets as close to the curb as he can but doesn't get out. It's a downpour outside. I step out of the car into a two foot deep puddle. I'm soaking wet by the time I run a couple of yards to the door."

When Landis gets inside, the bookstore is "a ghost town. It's a weeknight, and there's a tornado outside." By now, electricity is spotty, and there's no running water. The bookseller apologizes and, in the absence of functioning plumbing, expresses hope that Landis doesn't need to go to the bathroom.

Heigh ho, the glamorous life.

Not that good weather—nor even a good crowd—is any guarantee that you won't sit there alone and unloved at a signing. I once did a signing with Robin Wiete, a historical romance writer, a couple of weeks before Christmas. We were at a local author-friendly bookstore which had thoroughly publicized the event and ordered huge piles of our books for it. The shopping season, the fair weather that day, and the store's good location ensured there was heavy traffic in the store for the entire two hours Robin and I were there.

Neither of us sold a single book. And while we were there, someone actually came to the store to *return* a copy of one of Robin's books.

If you don't recognize Robin Wiete's name, by the way, it's because she later took a long sabbatical from the business to pursue a Ph.D. in psychology. One of her areas of interest is traumatic stress disorders. Coincidence? Maybe.

Anne Holmberg is another writer who knows how unpredictable signings can be: "I once signed books at a big book fair with Nora Roberts on one side and Nelson DeMille across the aisle. Just the three of us. Visions of glory danced in my head as I pictured a dozen pity sales, at least. But I did much better than that—I sold fully half the number of books that DeMille did, and seventy-five per cent of the books that Nora did!... DeMille sold six, Nora sold four, I sold three."

That reminds me of the time I let romance writer Toni Blake talk me into joining her at a statewide book fair, along with Teresa Medeiros, Elizabeth Bevarly, and several others. I wound up sitting next to a very loquacious self-published guy, and browsers kept picking up my books, then dropping them and backing away with puzzled or disdainful expressions on their faces.

I needed a cocktail *so* badly by the end of the day.

Writers are people who chose a profession, an art, a pursuit, a way of life that ensures that we spend most of our working lives alone. I mean, my idea of upgrading my workplace wardrobe was to buy several pairs of new pajamas last year; then another writer informed me I could order them online and not even leave the house to get them. And I'd never need to work again if I got a dollar every time a writer tells me how exhausted and drained she is after a conference, a signing, a workshop, a tour, or the Christmas holidays because there are *people* everywhere, and that's so tiring for someone used to spending every day alone in a room with her computer.

So it's doubly hard on a writer when public appearances turn out to be disappointing, depressing, or genuinely demeaning. I mean, actors and musicians *chose* that lifestyle, so they're supposed to live with that kind of crap. But we chose a lifestyle deliberately designed to *avoid* these scenarios—yet, somehow, like a clichéd nightmare, we inevitably wind up naked in public anyhow.

And speaking of being unclothed in public...

Former CPA Jodie Larsen had to attend a bar mitzvah on the same day she was scheduled to do a signing at a convention center. So Larsen dug up and donned an old pair of panty hose and high heels from her previous nine-to-five lifestyle, attended the ceremony, then rushed from the synagogue to the convention center. By mid-afternoon...the panty hose began to feel their age. As Larsen finished signing her books, "My panty hose slowly crept down until they were at mid-thigh level. After shaking hands with the men in the booth, I tried to waddle out, but it was impossible. Finally, I stopped in the aisle, kicked off my shoes, and rolled the darn things off. Three guys in another booth applauded as I put my shoes back on, blushed, and left as fast as humanly possible."

Lesson learned: Unlike fine wine, panty hose do not improve with time.

At yet another one of those signings where no one was buying books, novelist Dixie Browning was supervised by six representatives from the distributor who'd set up the signing. They were all male, all mid-thirties, and they all "stood behind me with their arms crossed over their chests." When Dixie took a powder-room break, she passed two women who'd noticed her six-man entourage. One of them said to the other, "She must be somebody important—she's got all those bodyguards."

I myself have never been mistaken for somebody important at a signing, though I have been mistaken for a bookstore employee, a bakesale hostess, and a loiterer.

When *New York Times* bestselling author Susan Elizabeth Phillips was on tour with *Kiss An Angel*, a Wal-Mart in Texas set her up in—where else?—the sportswear section. Right in front of a sale-rack of sweatshirts. They'd thoughtfully ordered a hundred copies of her previous book, but not one single copy of the book she was actually there to promote. As it turned out, this "was no tragedy because hardly any of the customers seemed to speak English—or only enough to ask me to find the sweatshirts for them in other sizes. I sold one book to a store employee in a pity buy."

Of course, the good thing about even a bad signing is that all you have to do is sit there quietly minding your own business. Whereas speaking engagements and public readings are minefields of potential embarrassment for writers.

The World Science Fiction Convention usually schedules "coffee klatches" for writers. It's a great idea for fans, who are the largest portion of convention attendees. Writers are scheduled to sit at a given table, usually large enough for at least a dozen people, and their readers can sign up to sit there and chat with them in a small group for an hour.

The first time I did a coffee klatch, one sole person showed up. And he was only there because he wanted to be at Hugo Award-winner Lois McMaster Bujold's nearby table, but it was full; he was hanging out at my table in the hopes that a seat would open up at hers.

I told him to go *open* one up. And then I went to the bar.

Novelist Carole Bellacera and two other writers once combined two evils by doing a signing along with a public reading. They read in the bookstore's café "to a bunch of people so rude they wouldn't even look up from their books." The only two people who even appeared to be listening actually got up and left in the middle of the program. "When our session was finished, no one even applauded. It was incredibly humiliating. I think, between the three of us, we sold four books."

I did a reading at a convention where only one person was in the audience—and he'd only come to hear the writer who was reading right after me.

Then again, you don't always want a lot of people present. In the middle one reading I did at a local bookstore, I had to explain to a friend's small daughter, in front of a decent-sized audience, that I appreciated her exuberant greeting but she needed to let go of my left breast now.

"Why?" she wanted to know.

When she is a teenager, I fully intend to torment her with this story.

Overall, I think we writers deserve a lot of credit for venturing out into the field, slogging through the trenches, and going public again and again, in support of our books, our work, our craft, year after year. We endure experiences which would make any rational person curl up in a fetal position and refuse ever again to expose herself to public abuse. Yet we tough it out and try again. Because we're brave? Because we're believers? Or because we have utterly flat learning curves? Maybe all of the above.

Much of the credit for our public *re*appearances, of course, goes to...the public. Not the public described in this article, but rather the public whose response to us makes us resilient enough to keep coming back.

Praise be to every reader who gushes gloriously about how much she loved your last book while getting you to autograph a copy of the brand new one. Raise your glass to every person who comes up to you after a reading, a speech, or a workshop to tell you how much she enjoyed it—and also to those people who, though they are too shy to speak to you, sit through your entire presentation in riveted silence with great eye contact. They, after all, make it worthwhile for us to venture forth into the cruel world of public appearances year after year.

How Long Does It Take?

I'm at a party minding my own business, when someone asks me, "How long does it take you to write a book?"

"Seven months, sixteen days, and forty-five minutes," I reply.

"No, really. How long?"

"Oh. You mean if I don't include all the trips to the bathroom and the coffee pot?"

❋

I'm at the doctor's office, exposing to a relative stranger those parts of myself which I normally only share with the most intimate of my acquaintances.

"So how long does it take you to write a book?"

I reply, "Not quite as long as you've had that instrument up my—"

"No, really. How long?"

"Oh. You mean if I include all the time I spend thinking about it?"

❋

After being put on hold for thirty-nine minutes, I am on the phone with an officer of the Internal Revenue Service. He cannot find my records, cannot help me with my problem, and cannot direct me to anyone who conceivably might help me with my problem.

When he finds out I'm a writer, he asks, "How long does it take you to write a book?"

"Not nearly as long as it takes me to get assistance from a federal civil servant."

"No, really. How long?"

"You mean if I leave out all the time I waste with the IRS?"

※

I am at dinner with a group of people I hardly know. An attractive man who paid no attention to me until learning that I am a writer asks (yeah, yeah, you can see it coming), "So how long does it take you to write a book?"

Arrrrrrggggggggggghhhhh!

This is one of the questions a writer is most frequently asked. And, frankly, it's a lot like being asked how long it takes you to have sex.

I mean, are you talking about a coed's backseat quickie on a night-better-forgotten during spring break? Or are you talking about a deeply in love couple on their second honeymoon in a secluded tropical paradise? Are you asking about a busy professional couple who've discovered their optimum moment for conceiving a child this month is during their lunchbreak in the middle of the workday? Or a couple who rarely get a whole hour alone together because they've got three small children? Or perhaps this same couple has just managed to find a babysitter and have checked into a nearby hotel for a weekend alone together? What about a couple where one partner is comforting another in a time of emotional crisis? Or two people who aren't a couple at all, and who'll never meet again? Or a husband and wife who've barely exchanged a civil word in five years, or a newly-in-love couple who can barely bear the eight hours per day that their jobs require them to be apart?

And so on.

I mean, it really depends on the individuals and the circumstances, doesn't it?

I once wrote a book in two weeks, start to finish. It was a 200-page manuscript, a fluffy piece of work-for-hire published under a pseudonym which I used only that one time. I enjoyed writing that book specifically *because* it was a short, easy book that required very little thought, depth, craftsmanship, complexity, or realism. I usually find my work difficult, and it was enjoyable to do something so fast and easy for a change, though I wouldn't want to make a career of it.

This does not mean, of course, that two weeks is how long it takes me to write a book. It's just how long it took me to write *that* book, due to its particular properties and circumstances.

At the other end of the spectrum, I spent nearly three years writing a fantasy novel. At 445,000 words, it was far and away the longest book I've ever written—or ever hope to write. (It was so long, in fact, that I wound up having to split it into two books, *The White Dragon* and *The Destroyer Goddess*.) It was also the most complex, difficult, layered, and challenging work I'd ever done up to that point.

I wrote its predecessor, *In Legend Born*, in roughly one year (but that novel was a mere 250,000 words). Back when I was writing series-romance novels for Silhouette Books under the pseudonym Laura Leone, I once wrote a book, *Guilty Secrets*, in about seventeen days (if you don't count the two outlines I wrote for it, which Silhouette didn't like and kept telling me to re-think). However, it was more typical for me to spend three or four months on a book for Silhouette—if we're counting rewrites and trips to the coffee pot. Nonetheless, I sold one book to them that took me seven months to write because of numerous difficulties I had with it. So if asked how long it took me to write a Silhouette, I'd have to say, "Seventeen days or seven months. It depends."

After leaving Silhouette, I wrote a 100,000-word contemporary romance novel for Kensington in about five months (or in two years, if you count the time I spent crossing all of Africa in between writing the proposal and then eventually selling and completing the book). There are some short stories I've written in a single two-hour sitting, and others which I've worked on for over a week.

My point—and I do have one—is that there is no "right" period of time which it "should" take to write a book. Each individual writer is different—and for some of us, even each individual project is different. While the person who simply never writes just isn't a writer (no matter what he may choose to call himself), the writer who writes v-e-r-y SLOWLY is no less a "writer" than the writer who delivers a polished novel every six weeks. (Many years ago, I did the math and worked out that Nora Roberts—today one of the bestselling writers in the world—was delivering, on average, a book every six weeks. I've lost count since then and don't know what her average is these days. Presumably it's slower, though, since her books have grown longer and more complex since those days.)

One of my favorite writers is extremely slow; yet I'd never want her to speed up if it meant sacrificing the quality of her work. The late Sarah Caudwell, a mystery writer, also produced very slowly; yet the four novels she wrote in her lifetime are among my most-often re-read keepers.

Which is not to imply that slower writers are therefore better writers. Another of my favorites, Elizabeth Peters a.k.a. Barbara Michaels, has been very prolific for many years.

Bottom line: It is a useless exercise to compare your pace with someone else's. I see writers doing it constantly, and it makes me despair—precisely because (write this down) it is a useless exercise to compare your pace with someone else's! I may envy someone who can write ten pages per day, five or six days per week, week after week—indeed, I *do* envy them, because I could get a lot more work into the marketplace if I wrote that fast. That does not mean, however, that such a person is a more valid or morally upstanding writer than I am, nor does it mean she's a *better* writer than I am. It just means she's faster. (She may indeed be a better writer than I, but her *speed* is not what makes her better.)

Meanwhile, of course, it's an insulting and arrogant literary myth that fast writing is bad writing, and that it takes at least five years (or whatever arbitrary timeframe someone suggests) to write a good book. What rubbish! It takes however long it takes that individual novelist to write that individual book. (I will assert, however, that you can't write a really good 445,000-word novel in seventeen days.)

To return to our analogy: Fifteen-minute sex at the right place and time with the right person can be great sex; two-hour sex with the wrong lover at the wrong place and time can be awful sex. (After all, there are some people on this planet you don't even want to be in the same *room* with for two hours, never mind exchange bodily fluids.) Someone can spend six weeks writing a delightful book; someone can spend seven years writing a piece of drek.

Speed primarily matters in terms of income and career building. Obviously, the person who can get a novel onto the book stands every six or twelve months has a good opportunity for marketplace momentum and (statistically) a better chance at career-building than someone who only gets one book out there every four years. The person who turns in three books per year probably has a better chance at making a living than the writer who turns in one book every two years.

However, the equation is, in reality, more complicated than that. A hardcover *New York Times* bestseller who turns in one sensationally successful book every three years makes much more money than a writer who turns in three neglected midlist paperbacks every year. If it takes you eighteen months to write a fabulous book that your publisher is very excited about, this is probably much better for your potential career growth than turning in a mediocre book every six months that makes absolutely *no one* excited.

The ideal might be (for example) to consistently deliver a highly successful novel twice a year. But it's a rare individual who can do that, just as it's a rare individual who can eat lots of chocolate and pizza without ever exercising, and yet never get fat. Yes, these individuals exist; but they're rare. We may well envy them (I certainly do), but it accomplishes nothing productive for us to condemn ourselves in comparison them.

You can, in most instances, take charge of how many hours per week you spend on your writing. You cannot, however, dictate whether you are the sort of person who feels

5,000-words-per-day eagerly rush through her and onto the page, or whether you're the sort who struggles hard to get two solid pages done in a focused three-hour stretch. Rather than waste time and energy castigating yourself for your natural pace, it would be wise to learn and acknowledge your pace, and then take steps to accommodate your individual needs and circumstances.

For example, if you can't write a book in ten-minute spurts of time as the kids wander in and out of your office, then work out a system with your family whereby you can get (say) two uninterrupted hours per day four days per week. If you can't produce fifty pages every single week even while writing full-time alone at home five days per week, it's probably not going to improve your productivity to worry that another writer's pace is faster. If you're steadily producing 800 words per day, take pleasure in this reliable and productive pace, rather than fretting that it's not four times faster than that. I once knew a bestselling writer who hit such a rough period, she would have been *thrilled* to get one full page per day written. Eventually, things improved, and she reached that goal and surpassed it. But there was a time when, even for that very successful writer, everyone else's pace seemed enviable.

Meanwhile, if you happen to be one of those rare people who can consistently write fifteen pages a day, five days per week, week after week—and if it's all good material—then don't ever take that ability for granted. Many of us would actually pay big annual fees (or even dance with the devil) to have a similar pace.

Jabla

West Africa, in the 1990s. I'm on the outskirts of Bamako, the colorful and chaotic capital city of Mali, one of the poorest nations in the world. We make our camp in the ruins of the Lido, a small hotel destroyed by fire during the riots two years earlier. By night, I sleep on the veranda of the gutted building, surrounded by flowering vines and trees full of singing birds.

At the bottom of the wooded hill on which the hotel sits, there's a beautiful pond, perfect for swimming, with rocks for diving and sunbathing. The little cascades running into the cool water are enough to make me rationalize that this is *moving* water and therefore okay for swimming in.

Many bodies of water in Africa contain dangerous parasites, deadly diseases, and cranky wildlife, so it's unwise to go near water that isn't well known for being safe. The realities of living in the bush, however, soon alter a person's standards. A month later, for example, I will launder my mud-caked clothing in a river where people get killed by crocodiles on a regular basis; by then, this will seem like an acceptable risk to me.

Anyhow, hot, tired, and intensely dirty after having crossed the Sahara Desert (not to mention spending considerable time digging our vehicle *out* of the Sahara Desert), I throw caution to the wind and join my companions swimming in the pond hidden in the jungle near the Lido. And it's fabulous! This is the first time I've been cool in weeks and the first time I've been clean in over a month.

Then a small group of locals comes along. They are led by an old man who has no teeth and speaks almost no French (officially, the common language of West Africa; in reality, not always useful). The old man warns me, the only French speaker in the group, that this water has jabla and is therefore terribly dangerous.

Jabla, I ask?

The old man tries to explain, but his lack of teeth affects his articulation, and he doesn't seem to be using many French words, anyhow. He grows increasingly agitated over my lack of comprehension and insists we *must* get out of the water, we're in terrible danger, we're all going to die. The jabla is very bad, he tells me, and a number of people are dead because of it—two of them died just last year, in fact.

Yes, but what *is* jabla, I ask? A disease? A parasite? A crocodile? An evil spirit? A venomous snake? Drowning? A vengeful curse? A local joke invented to get rid of unkempt white people?

Because of the language barrier, I can't find out what jabla is; but the old man's conviction that it'll kill us convinces us to get out of the water.

I spend the next two weeks wondering exactly what I'm going to die of, and how soon. Are we talking about something

as severe as snail fever, for example, which you get from contact
with the wrong water and which really *will* kill me if I don't
get myself to a Western hospital for expensive treatment right
away? Or is jabla some kind of demon that I don't even believe
in? Did I escape jabla when I got out of the water alive and
unharmed? Or is jabla already in my bloodstream and attack-
ing my nervous system? And, if so, how soon before it kills me?

This is what's so damn distressing about jabla. You don't
know what causes it or what its initial symptoms are. You don't
know if someone *else's* mysterious undiagnosed illness is jabla
or something else entirely. You don't know if you've got jabla
within you and just don't realize it yet. And you don't know
how—or even *if*—you can get cured once you discover jabla has
infected you.

Oh, yeah, jabla is a bitch.

But, hey, you don't need me to tell *you* about jabla. You
know all about it. After all, you're a writer.

My first exposure to jabla was not in Africa. It was when I
was an aspiring writer, awaiting news of my first submission at
Silhouette by day and writing my fourth manuscript by night.
While exploring the fiction pond in the publishing jungle, I
noticed many writerly corpses near the water. This sparked a
dark, boundless fear in me.

For example, at garage sales and second-hand bookstores, I
kept coming across tattered ten-year-old paperback books with
cover blurbs touting them as "The Incredible International
Bestseller! Nineteen Weeks on the *New York Times* list!" And in
most cases, I had never heard of the authors, nor could I find
any in-print fiction by those writers. Additionally, there were
numerous romance writers (romance being the genre I was trying to break into) who seemed to have disappeared off the face

of the planet after a few books, and I was plagued by morbid suspicions about this. I thought it seemed unlikely that they'd *all* died suddenly or gone to Rio, even if a few of them had.

That's jabla: "What in the world *happened* to that missing writer, and—the key question—can it happen to *me*?"

In fact, that instance of jabla got chased away when I had the opportunity to meet one of these writers. She'd sold three books. The third one had not been a happy editorial experience, and her fourth book got rejected. After that, she never wrote or submitted a book again.

In other words, jabla never even got a *chance* to get her, because when she went into the water, she tied rocks to her feet and went down without a struggle.

Since then, despite being dumped by publishers and having others fold beneath me, I have never seriously feared disappearing. Because ever since then, the explanation for the disappearances of writers seems practical and self-evident to me, no longer a dark mystery with a sinister name for which I have no real definition. I learned that writers disappear when they stop writing and submitting, writing and submitting, writing and submitting.

Simple cause and effect, not jabla.

But when something goes terribly wrong for a working writer, other writers are often spooked by it. I know because *I* get spooked. And also because my own career has spooked people. When I was dumped by Silhouette after eleven books, for example, other Silhouette writers peppered me with questions, trying to find symptoms which would either confirm or negate the possibility of their having my disease. Similarly, when another writer delivers a book which the editor declares unacceptable and won't pay for, I usually pepper the writer with questions, trying to define a set of circumstances I could take steps to avoid in my own career. When another writer's sales decline and she's advised to change her pen name if she wants to keep working, I want to know what the first signs of trouble were so that I can examine my own career for them.

When someone, despite writing and submitting, writing and submitting, writing and submitting, can't get work, I interrogate him if I get the chance, eager to discover a pattern which I can learn not to emulate. And when a previously steady or prolific writer burns out or comes up against the wall of writer's block—jabla alert! I'm not the only writer wondering, "Why her and not me? How did she catch it, and how can I make sure I *don't* catch it?"

When a writer dries up, or when she keeps writing but no one will buy her work anymore, or when someone who was once a star can now barely sell a book...Oh, yes, that makes for big, hairy, long-fanged writer jabla. That's the darkest, ugliest jabla of all: "Is what killed that writer going to kill me, too?"

I'm something of an expert on this because I thought about jabla a *lot* when I was mired in my 1,732-page fantasy opus which was released as a two-volume epic, *The White Dragon* and *The Destroyer Goddess* (how's that for titling the story that nearly killed me?).

Until writing that story, I had never experienced writer's block and had never given it much thought. But the long-term paralysis I experienced on that book was a wake-up call from hell, and I learned that it can indeed happen here—because it happened here for at least eighteen months. I spent so long unable to write a single word on that book that I was surprised when a friend recently told me it had never occurred to her that I might not finish it. The possibility of never finishing it

occurred to *me* all of the time. Every damn day for well over
a year. The fear made me sick. When I only had sixty pages
completed more than a year after the book's due date, you *bet*
it occurred to me that I might never finish it.

That was probably the nadir of my professional life, those
many long months that I spent burned out and trying to get
that damn book to lift off. I couldn't get anything *else* to lift
off, either, while that book hung around my neck like a dead
albatross. And I had written fourteen novels before this! How
could this happen to me? *Me*, a prolific workhorse who'd
always thought writer's block and creative burn-out were things
that happened only to *other* people?

Jabla finally got me.

In truth, many tangible factors contributed to my lengthy,
blank-minded, terrified standstill on that book. But one of
them, I eventually realized, was my unwitting focus on the
final, polished result which I wanted the reader to encounter
when opening that novel. I discovered that it's way too easy
for a writer to lose sight of the story she wants to tell, and to
think instead of the story she wants the reader to read. It's
surprisingly seductive for the writer to get mired in thoughts of
the effect which she wants the final, polished, completed novel
to have on people. I was doing this, and it was a significant
factor in scaring me into sheer paralysis, because no single
sentence or scene I could craft on any given workday could
equal the overall completed novel in which I wanted the reader
to become engrossed.

Every journey is made step by step, and every book must
be written moment by moment. The tricky part, of course, is
that we have to balance the individual moments with the *whole*
project in our head, or all we get is gobbledygook. But I can't

Jabla **2 0 3**

sit down to the *whole* project and write it, because then I just freak out. I know this. I've known it ever since I discovered it while writing my first book. Yet many books later, I forgot this basic tenet of my craft, and I freaked out when I sank into the quagmire, early in the process of writing that novel, of thinking about the book I wanted the reader to read, rather than the story I wanted to write.

Comedian Mike Myers has said, "One of the deaths of creativity is being results-oriented, having any sort of expectation or attachment. What you have to do is just focus on what you're working on."

I knew that.

So my long period of writer's block wasn't jabla, after all. There was an explanation for it so self-evident, I could just punch myself.

Not only did it take me many months to identify and shed this problem, but I'm still wrestling with it today. It's the antagonist which will not die. However, I didn't originally define this form of jabla by diagnosing myself. No, I'd originally recognized it when talking with another writer, someone who had successfully written short pieces and who wanted to write a novel. He knew exactly what story he wanted to tell. But he paralyzed himself with fear by focusing on how he wanted the book to be perceived by readers and critics. We talked about it at length because, in someone *else*, this problem was as obvious to me as a dead elephant on Madison Avenue. I mean, you look at it and say, "Gosh, that dead pachyderm doesn't belong there!"

It took me a lot longer, though, to realize when *I* was inflicting the same paralyzing burden on my own creative process. Now that I've caught myself in the act, I wish I could find the secret formula for never letting myself do it again—but at least I'm getting better about monitoring myself in this respect. And I know it isn't jabla, after all. I'm not going to die of it. Not just yet.

There's some wise advice out there that has helped me shake off this phenomenon when it happens. One piece of it comes from Susan Sontag, who once said that while writing *The Volcano Lover,* she kept thinking it was a bad novel, but she figured (I paraphrase): "Oh, well, everyone's entitled to a bad novel now and then, so I'll just keep writing." So now, when I become paralyzed with fear over how brilliant my work-in-progress *isn't,* I force myself to repeat that phrase and just keep writing. Similarly, a quote which romance novelist Julie Kistler has shared with me is: "The first step to get past writer's block is to lower your standards."

I've also learned to tell myself, "Look, when you finish the book and it sucks canal water, you can buy it back, so no one will ever find out what drivel it is. But, first, you have to finish it." And a non-writing friend of mine taught me this mantra: "If a thing is worth doing, then it's worth doing badly." As opposed to not doing it at all for fear of not doing it perfectly.

Anyhow, here's the thing that years in this business and years at this keyboard have taught me about jabla: Its real power over us is fear. My swim in the jungle near the Lido only lasted about twenty minutes; but I spent every day of the next two weeks being scared. *That's* jabla.

Let's Face the Music

Way back in my Silhouette days, I got stuck on a book and couldn't continue writing it. This was problematic, since the deadline was approaching and I was already behind schedule. I just couldn't figure out what the story was about. I had characters, setting, plot, and conflict, but they felt like a jumble of elements; I didn't understand the story's heart, only its limbs.

So I walked around for days like a madwoman, muttering to myself over and over, "What's this damn book about?" I asked this question as I showered, as I cleaned house, as I did laundry, bought groceries, drove around town on my errands, phoned the IRS, and so on.

On the third day of this mental pacing, I walked past a pony keg (which is local slang for a shop that sells wine and beer). It was a nice day, and the shop's sound system was blaring out of their open door. I walked past the door, obsessing about my problem: "What's the book about?"

And, floating out of the pony keg, the voice of Don

Henley, who was one of the Eagles, was singing a song from his solo album *The End of Innocence*, in which he advised me that "it's about forgiveness."

Eureka!

Don was right! That's exactly what *The Bandit King* was about. Forgiveness was the heart of that book. And without that song pointing it out to me in a serendipitous moment, who knows how much longer it would have taken me to figure it out?

Nor is that the only thanks I owe to Henley. A year or two later, I got the double-entendre title of my award-winning Silhouette, *Untouched By Man*, from listening to the title song of his *End of Innocence*. Similarly, I got the title of a short story, "Heaven's Only Daughter" (which appeared in a DAW Books anthology called *Whatdunits*), from Paul Simon's brilliant album, *The Rhythm of the Saints*. A song in that album also inspired the plot line in another Silhouette I wrote, *The Black Sheep*, when the characters decide to try to save the little harbor church of Saint Cecilia (the patron saint of music).

Considering my modest earnings, however, I do not fear that Henley and Simon will demand a cut of those back-royalties.

I wrote *Fallen From Grace*, a romance novel, on a tight schedule, squeezing it between fantasy novels. Without constantly playing the soundtrack of *Tous Les Matins Du Monde*, a French film about 17th century musicians, I don't know how I could have written that book. I also like to listen to Bach, Mozart, and Handel when I write. The elegant, precise, and slightly exotic tones of Baroque music help me focus my mind on my work even when I'm panicking about looming deadlines for multiple commitments in a short span of time.

I listened to *Between Earth and Sky* by Rhea's Obsession so much while writing *The White Dragon* that I discovered I couldn't proofread the copy edit of the book without putting that CD back in the stereo. I hadn't listened to Rhea's Obsession in months, and once again hearing the exotic, passionate, melodic, and faintly brutal semi-Celtic music of this Canadian band put me right back in the saddle of that book, able to assess the copy editor's work without ambivalence or hesitation. It was as if I had never been through the period of months when I *wasn't* totally immersed in that book's prose every day. The galleys for the book later arrived without warning (of course), and I had to proofread them while visiting friends in another city. So, naturally, I took the Rhea's Obsession CD with me.

As it happens, this seems to be ordinary—dare I even say *normal?*—behavior among writers. Bestselling romance novelist Teresa Medeiros says that finding the right music for a book kick-starts her brain: "Once I find that magical piece of music, I will play it over and over until the cats and my husband run screaming from the room. I actually find myself typing to its rhythm, and if I've been away from the story for a few days, the music will pull me right back in it. It's as if it acts as the key to my subconscious." (I picture Terri's cats fleeing the room with expressions of mad horror on their little whiskered faces.)

Writer Lillian Stewart Carl plays the same music for a book over and over, too, and says, "I can pick up books I wrote 10-12 years ago and remember the music I was listening to at the time!" Novelist Madeline Baker got hooked on the *Braveheart* soundtrack this way for a while. Writer Janelle Burnham Schneider finds that silence lets her brain wander too much, whereas music keeps her focused. Gail Link describes herself as "a writer who *needs* music to set the mood...When I find a piece that fits what I'm working on, I use it over and over, ad nauseum." She got into this habit when writing her very first book, *Wolf's Embrace*, when she repeatedly played an album by the Irish group Clannad.

Come to think of it, before I started playing Rhea's Obsession to death while writing *White Dragon*, I was playing Clannad to death for several hundred pages.

Bestseller Kay Hooper finds that something about the rhythm of Gregorian chanting helps her concentrate. (Me, too. Gregorian chants work well when I want something playing in the background but find myself listening too much to "real" music.)

Many writers who write to music cite the "right" music as being a key issue for them, using music to help them find the mood or tone of a novel. "I pick a composer for each book, one whose work I think echoes the tone and theme of the story," says Tracy Grant. She adds that she doesn't listen exclusively to that composer, however, because it takes her a year or so to write a book, and she'd go nuts without any variety during that time. Since it takes me a long time to write a fantasy novel, I need a little variety, too. In fact, even on *Fallen From Grace*, which was a mere leaflet of 480 manuscript pages, I switched CDs about halfway through the book, finally growing tired of the first one. Novelist P.G. Nagle uses music not only to set the mood for a whole book, but also for specific scenes: "Battle music for battle scenes, folk songs for folksy scenes, etc." Karyn Witmer-Gow says, "Love scenes, especially tender love scenes, require Barber's 'Adagio for Strings.'"

Though Sylvie Kurtz will play a particular CD over and over again if it's helping her break through a bout of writer's block, she usually prefers silence. Romance writer Candace Schuler usually plays mellow jazz in the background, though she says that neither silence nor noise make a difference on the all-too-rare occasions when she's in the "zone" and too deeply immersed in the work to hear anything else. (I have been in that zone maybe twice.)

Though bestseller Jo Beverley will use music (often chosen to suit the era or the tone of a novel) to block out intrusive noise, she usually writes in silence. Australian writer Sherry-Anne Jacobs also prefers to write in silence, because modern noise jars her when writing historicals. Jean Brashear also prefers silence, finding that music influences the mood of her work *too* much, actually getting between her and her characters. Though Annette Carney likes the *idea* of finding the right music for each project, it doesn't work for her in practice: "The music seems to take up all the space in my head," and she therefore prefers silence, too. Having also had trouble with the whole "background music" experiment, romance novelist Dixie Browning says she has nonetheless found one CD that goes with everything: Tommy Emmanuel's solo album, *Only*.

Katherine Garbera first started writing at work when she was a receptionist and therefore can't write in silence (so she plays music), but Ann Roth, Melanie Jackson, and Toni Blake are all members of the "silence is golden" contingent. Blake adds that the passage of time has only made her more adamant about needing silence to work. Pat Roy *dreams* of silence as she tries to hear herself think above the noise of children, dogs, and football announcers. After years of writing books with three small children in the house, Judith Bowen says that now, "I need silence!" She prefers to write in an empty house, while the kids are at school and the dogs are asleep—and adds that she'll even cover the bird's cage if necessary. She also uses earplugs to ensure silence for her concentration. And she's not the only one to do so; when someone else is in Suzanne Simmons' house, or when lawn mowers are disturbing her concentration, she, too, relies on earplugs.

Though I normally prefer music when working, I rely on earplugs on days when I can hear a lawn mower outside of every damn window of my home and can't ignore the grating roar that cuts across the music I'm playing. I also resort to earplugs on the occasions when my next door neighbor's teenage son blares rap music from a CD player while working on his car in the driveway below my windows. And I relied on earplugs often when I had upstairs neighbors whose daily habits were so noisy that I could scarcely hear my stereo above the thumping, crashing, and smashing that occurred round the clock. (They moved before I could kill them.)

Although Cheryl Wolverton prefers silence when she's writing at night, by day she enjoys movie soundtracks. One of the ones she mentions is *Last of the Mohicans*, which Karyn Witmer-Gow describes as "the all-time best writing music." A *lot* of fantasy writers love that one, too, including me.

Thriller writer Ronn Kaiser says he gave up listening to background music years ago, since he falls into a meditative trance when writing which makes him oblivious to what's going on around him. He does add, however, that one could say he writes to "white noise," given that his old, noisy computer sounds like a washing machine.

In fact, "white noise" is pretty popular with a number of writers. Although all man-made noises pull Sue Pace out of the story, she likes the sound of rain falling on the roof or a waterfall splashing outside an open window. Lauren Bach, who used to need total silence to write, has found her productivity enhanced by playing a CD of ocean waves. Meanwhile, music lover Janelle Burnham Schneider is particularly fond of a CD that mingles soft instrumental music with the sound of a waterfall. I have a Sound Soother, a little audio device that makes sounds like waves, rain, or a babbling brook. Silence almost never works for me, so I have found the Sound Soother particularly useful for days when my concentration is so fragile that any music, even Gregorian chanting or Baroque cellos, distracts me.

In a twist that I do not hesitate to call eccentric, Robin Bayne refers to the QVC channel on cable TV as "great white noise for writing." (I would shoot the television after twenty minutes.) Lynn Miller and Annette Mahon are two more writers who can write to the noise of the TV, though both say they prefer music, particularly instrumental music, i.e. without lyrics.

Indeed, the vast majority of novelists who write to music seem to prefer music without lyrics. As Colleen Thompson says, "When I'm at the keyboard, songs with audible, understandable language interfere with my own flow of words." So, like me, she has different tastes in music, based on whether or not she's writing to it. With few exceptions, I prefer music without lyrics or (to borrow a phrase from Colleen) Music With Incomprehensible Lyrics when I'm writing; and, when I'm not writing, I usually prefer music with lyrics that I can listen to.

One notable exception to this common preference, however, is novelist Phoebe Conn, who describes Janice Joplin as her all-time favorite music for writing. "If I can get her pain in my prose, then I know my reader will sob along with my characters." Certainly, there are many singers and lyric songs I've heard in my head while I work, even if I rarely *play* them while working.

As we've seen here, there are writers who need complete silence to work—and their professional accomplishments are evidence enough that they certainly know what they need for their process. However, I myself couldn't work without music, at least not as a regular habit. Music stimulates, soothes, inspires, and focuses me. I consider it a mainstay of my writing process—as, I've now learned, many other novelists do, too. I owe a huge debt of gratitude to the hundreds of composers and musicians who, through their art, their craft, and their talent, have made possible the development of my own.

The Artist's Knife

Every time I feel that I can't catch a break in my career, or that brick buildings keep falling on me, or that I've got a *right* to sing the blues...it helps me to remember that no one ever said this would be easy. In fact, I'm pretty sure everyone always promised me exactly the opposite.

The writer's wilderness is no place for the faint-hearted. This life isn't easy, and (newsflash!) it's not supposed to be. So get over it. Or, as the saying goes, "If you're afraid of wolves, keep out of the woods."

Do the estimates of how many aspiring writers never publish a word frighten you? Do you hate seeing the statistics about how many professional writers never sell a fourth novel (or even a second one)? Do you feel sick with nerves when you hear the words "midlist crunch?" Do you get a stress migraine every time you hear yet another story of someone whose editor told her that her recently delivered manuscript was "unpublishable" and would be neither paid for nor released?

Well, here's an open secret: Me, too.

When I first started writing, back in the late 1980s, was I daunted by the statistics of how many unsolicited manuscripts flooded romance publishers? Good God, yes! What am I, stupid? You think I can't count? However, as *Jonathan Livingston Seagull* author Richard Bach says, "A professional writer is an amateur who didn't quit." Given the alternative (quitting), I chose to work as hard as I could on developing my craft, researching the market, and pursuing publication. Novelist John Jakes was right: "Too many beginning writers give up too easily."

I significantly improved my odds just by not giving up. And so can you.

A few months after I sold my first book, I attended my first-ever romance genre event. There were several published writers giving brief speeches, followed by a reception. I sat next to a woman who had completed nine manuscripts. *Nine*! Wow! It would be several more years before I completed my ninth novel.

But I was already a professional writer, and she wasn't. Talent may have been a factor, but the most important reason she'd never sold a word was...she had never submitted any of those manuscripts anywhere. Not even one. If she submitted a book, she explained to me, then she might be rejected! And she couldn't bear that!

"Well, writing is a wonderful hobby," I said, "and you obviously enjoy it a great deal."

On the contrary, she protested! She wasn't content to be a hobbyist! She had every intention of becoming a professional!

"But...if you won't risk rejection," I ventured, "how can you possibly sell a book?"

She evidently hadn't worked that one out yet, and I somehow came away feeling I'd been tactless.

Let's be very clear about this: Rejection is part of the

profession. There's no way around it. Every writer deals with it differently, but the key phrase here is *every writer deals with it*.

Rejection is a common artistic fear, of course. For the novelist, it usually comes in a letter. When you get a form rejection, you're frustrated by the lack of specific information. When you get an editorial rejection, you're wounded by the specific comments. It's a lose-lose situation. Here's another open secret: I feel sick every time I get a rejection.

Yes, I know, some writers say you shouldn't let rejection upset or depress or wound you. Well, gosh, it must be nice to have control over what you find upsetting, depressing, or wounding. Me, I have no such luck. If something hurts or upsets me, it just *does*. And don't come around me with that "should/shouldn't" crap unless you want me to punch you.

If you're genuinely afraid of rejection (or bad reviews, or horrific revisions, or being dumped by a publisher, or being cut loose by an agent, or freezing up during a workshop) here's a tip I learned way back in my days as an apprentice at the Williamstown Theatre Festival. Our acting teacher used to urge us to confront stage fright, fear of ridicule, fear of auditioning, and numerous other common acting fears by imagining the very worst thing that could possibly happen. *Really* picture it! In *detail*. And then *deal* with it. It's a kind of desensitizing process of the imagination, a mental exercise similar to those which psychologists do with people who suffer from traumatic stress disorders or phobias.

This is tough love at its most diabolical.

Just as the artist's knife scrapes, folds, and carves one's talent and vision into a masterpiece, the writer must find her own inner knife to refine, regroup, and dig deep when challenges arise and plans flounder. The writer must carve her talent into work that builds her career. Sometimes, in the process, she even has to toss out the baby along with the bathwater and start all over again. This isn't a pity party. This is the island where you need to be much stronger than those folks on *Survivor*. This is a wilderness where anything could jump out of the jungle to eat you alive at any time. And you can significantly improve your odds of surviving—nay, thriving!—by keeping your knife sharpened and ready at all times.

Sound grim? It's not. I had an epiphany about this while watching a TV interview with Kurt Russell a few years ago. Russell was a child actor whose real ambition was to play pro baseball—and he did, briefly, before getting an injury that ended his sports career. So, with his plans turned to ashes, Russell turned to the only other career he knew: acting. Ultimately, as we know, he became an extremely successful actor.

When my modest series-romance career turned to ashes in the early 1990s, I turned to writing other things...and thereby became a single-title romance writer, an award-winning science fiction/fantasy short story writer, a hardcover epic fantasy novelist, and so on. I also tried my hand at nonfiction and sold a few travel articles. This is not to say that everything I touched turned to gold. It didn't. I also tried (and failed at) several other possible avenues of writing. What I *didn't* do was sit around moaning about my bad luck. What I didn't do was give up.

After a career upset, some writers find new work right away, and some take years to find new work. The ones who *never again* find work are the ones who give up. It's that simple.

But let's get back to Kurt Russell. When he turned to acting after leaving baseball, he initially just regarded it as a working career, something he could do for a living.

What changed Russell's attitude about acting and turned it into a passion for him was—wait for it!—*failure*. He made a TV movie called *Elvis: The Movie* in which he played the king of rock. A number of critics slammed his performance. In the interview I watched years later, Russell said when he suddenly realized acting was *risky*, something he could *fail* at, *that's* when it became interesting to him. *That's* when it became a passion, an exciting prospect full of inherent rewards he had not previously perceived.

Lightning bolt! Epiphany!

Ever since seeing that interview, that's the way I try (with varying degrees of success) to view the artistic and emotional risks of our profession. After all, I don't want to be downtrodden, embittered, and unhappy; but neither can I pretend to myself (or to you) that this is a kind and generous profession (by and large, it's a ruthless and unforgiving one). So I adopted the viewpoint that Kurt Russell introduced to me:

The potential for failure is, in effect, what makes it so worth doing.

Because if it were easy, then anyone could do it. I don't want to be just *anyone*, and neither do you. I want to be a woman who runs with wolves—and that means going into the woods which, as Robert Frost knew, are lovely, but also dark and deep. It means going to the edge, and occasionally even jumping *off* the edge without a safety net or a parachute. It means flying west with the night, into the unknown, and trusting in yourself to get there intact—or to be strong enough to survive and regroup if you go down in flames.

So someone rejected your book? Send it out again. *Everyone* rejected your book? Write another. The rejections are wounding? They usually are. The reviews are painful? Been there, done that.

Your career crashed and burned, and now no one will even answer your calls?

Okay, pop quiz: Do you lie there whimpering and bemoaning your bad luck for the next five years, or do you figure out what else you can write and then go write it?

I write a lot of different things, and versatility is one of the key reasons I've never been out of work for long. Here's a tip about versatility: *It's all hindsight.* Every single time I say to an editor, "Sure, I can do that," I'm lying. It's only after it's done that I discover I really *can* do it.

The first time I sat down to write a series-romance novel, I knew I couldn't do it. When I signed for my first single-title romance, *Fever Dreams*, I knew I couldn't do it. When I sold my first epic fantasy novel, I *really* knew I couldn't do it. My first short story (and my second, and my sixth, and my tenth), my first article (and my third, and my eighth), my first column, my first whatever…These were all things I knew for a fact I couldn't do. And in every single case, I did them. I committed emphatically to doing them, giving myself little choice but to leave the country if I *didn't* then do them.

The words "yes, I can" require courage (or a compulsive desire to keep working) in a writer…as well as, okay, a rather flexible view of truth in advertising. The words "I can't do that" are a self-fulfilling prophecy, whether it's "I can't bear rejection," or "I can't write a different kind of novel than the ones I've always written."

Now I know some shrewd writers out there are shaking their heads as they read this and saying, "But what about career planning?" That's a good point. Suffice it to say that, no, you really shouldn't take every contract that comes your way, or pursue every single potential opportunity you hear about, or write all over the map. Indeed not. Focus and career planning are indeed important.

But the one thing you can never afford to do as an artist is to limit your options, opportunities, and accomplishments out of *fear*.

So picture the worst thing that can happen to you, imagine your very worst fear as an artist—and *deal* with it. Learn to view the potential for failure as the risk that makes a thing *worth* doing. Practice the words "yes, I can," and say them when you secretly mean, "I really want to, but I know I can't."

I significantly improve my odds of surviving in this profession just by learning to do it scared. And so can you.

Habit Forming

I've tried cigarettes a few times—and I've never once under-stood the attraction. I've spent enough of my life standing downwind of smoking campfires, thanks, so I feel no need to light up a cigarette to reproduce the effect. Especially since I'm not at my most pleasant when I'm red-faced, teary-eyed, and gasping for air.

However, I think the real reason I'm not a smoker, apart from my general enjoyment of breathing, is that I lack the discipline to form the habit. To become a real smoker—some-one who can indeed call it a *habit*—you need to light up at least ten times a day, wouldn't you say? And truly dedicated smokers—chain smokers, the real elite of smokerdom—have to do it, what, once every twenty minutes?

Me, I've been known to forget to *inhale* on occasion, so I doubt I could cope with the demands of having to remember to locate and light a cigarette that often. You think I'm being facetious (I can see it in your eyes), but there was actually a period in my childhood when I so frequently forgot to inhale that I was constantly passing out in a dead faint; even now, I still sometimes get quite dizzy before I remember to breathe. So perhaps you can see how someone like me could go deep into nicotine withdrawal without figuring out what was wrong.

I'm just not good at habits. As soon as I form one, I get tired of it, or simply find myself incapable of maintaining it. To be regular about anything—even a *bad* habit—is more effort, more discipline, than I can muster.

Consider: To be a smoker, you not only have to remember to light up once every sixty minutes (for example), you also have to remember to keep yourself supplied with cigarettes and matches and places to drop your ashes and put your stubs. See how complicated it's getting already? Then if you're *me*, you'd invariably run out of cigarettes at three o'clock in the morning in a strange city right after your rental car blew up, and the sheer overwhelming *pressure* to remain true to your habit in the face of such obstacles would be monumentally destructive.

Which is why, as I've matured, I've shed all guilt and concern about not being a creature of habit. I've decided it's just my little way of ensuring that I don't someday find myself hitch hiking in Poughkeepsie at 3:00 AM in search of Virginia Slims.

It's also why I utterly loathe, hate, despise, and dread the inevitable questions about my "habits" as a writer.

You know the questions I mean: Do you write every day? How many hours per day do you write? How many pages per day do you write? Do you research before you start the book, or while you're working on the book? How much research do you do? How long does it take you to write a book? Do you have any rituals when you sit down to write? Do you know everything that will happen before you write a scene, or does it all come as a surprise to you? What do you do about writer's block? How long is a chapter? Do you see the characters or the plot first? Does setting arise from story, or story from setting? How many angels can dance on the head of a pin?

I DON'T KNOW.

Well, no, I'm lying. Gee, here's a big cat to let out of the bag: I do not write every day.

I probably think about writing every day. In my mind's eye, I dream of an ideal Laura Resnick who writes every day. (She also exercises daily, manages money well, rarely loses her temper, and eats a high-fiber low-fat diet.) I don't necessarily sneer at writers who say things like, "Writing is a muscle, and you need to exercise it every day." I often punish myself for not writing every day. I occasionally neglect to correct total strangers who simply assume I write every day.

But, no, I don't write every day. And if I ever do, then you'll probably need to expose and arrest the person masquerading as me. Because, hullo!, writing every day qualifies as a *habit*, and I don't have any. We've already been all through this—pay attention!

However, since I know lots of writers who don't write every day, I don't get too touchy about this question. Besides, *no* is an easy answer. Short. Succinct. To the point.

It's all those other questions that drive me bonkers. And my bonkerism increases ten-fold when other *writers* ask me this stuff. In general, I think that "how writers write" is a topic right up there with laundry products for sheer lack of scintillation. However, novelist Harry Turtledove woke me up to the facts of life in an article he wrote for the *SFWA Bulletin,* the quarterly magazine of the Science Fiction Writers of America, when he compared writing to sex: Everyone (Harry said) wants to know how everyone else does it.

Ah-hah! My problem in a nutshell—I don't want to know how my friends and enemies (let alone my relatives or my colleagues) have sex. Not ever. I mean, please, I can accept, in a purely abstract way, that you have sex; but I never ever want to have even *one* mental image of you having sex, or vice versa. Line drawn, door closed, cut to the waves pounding against the shore, and FADE OUT.

Similarly...sorry, all my esteemed fellow writers, but I really don't give a damn how any of you write your books. Not Kathy Eagle, whose books are so moving that I often want to quit writing after I read them. Not Nora Roberts, who writes so prolifically and successfully that she constitutes a genuine phenomenon. Not Mary Jo Putney, one of my wisest and favorite writing friends. No matter how much I respect the person, love the work, or envy the success, I have no interest in hearing or reading about or discussing the *process*. Everyone makes love in their own way; and the key words there, in my opinion, are *in their own way*.

I'm often flabbergasted when I hear about how someone else writes a book. Multiple drafts? (I'd quit in exhausted despair.) Graphs and charts and right-angle juxtaposition? (I was always bad at geometry.) Everything planned in advance, all factors known and accounted for before composing the prose. (I'd never feel compelled to write if I already knew everything that would happen.) Scenes written at random, then later put in order and quilted together. (How does one even *do* that?)

I'm usually equally aghast at people's (unrequested) descriptions of their sex lives: You do *what* to get in the mood? You did it *where*? He asked for *what*? And this was *how* many people? But didn't the latex itch after a while? Well, why don't you just *tell* him that you're bored and counting ceiling tiles? Wait, this wasn't the feather boa *I* loaned you, was it?

I'm also regularly bowled over by the work habits that writers come out of the closet with: Writing from 4:00 AM to 7:00 AM. (Sorry, I'm busy REMing at that time.) Writing ten pages a day everyday no matter what. (The number of friends whom I've had to coax out of the "I'm so inadequate, I'm such a fraud!" doldrums after hearing *that* one...) Writing on separate projects in the morning and the afternoon. Writing without leaving a room for weeks. Writing in public, in private, by hand, with voice-operated software, without music, with one specific piece of music playing non-stop, with the TV on, with the blinds drawn, with candles burning, with cookies at hand, outside, inside, at the beach, on a laptop, in a laundry room...

And what have you learned, Dorothy?

Everyone's different. So there's no "right" way. Ergo, no one can give you the answers, whether you're a dreamy-eyed aspirant who has yet to complete even one short story, or the burned-out veteran of fifty novels looking to refresh yourself. It's like sex. Once in a while, someone may have a specific gem of advice that will help you find the path to fulfillment, but mostly—whether writing or making love—you just have to muddle through by yourself (or with your collaborator, shall we say), in an open-hearted trial-and-error quest, and find your own way of doing what you need to do in order to get what you want.

And if you're someone who can't ever get into the habit of forming habits, like me, then your writing process is always changing. Which is why I can never answer those damn questions about how I write. I don't know how many pages a day I write, or how many hours a day I sit here, or what daily goals I

set, or what I know (or don't know) at the start of a project or
a scene, or how much research I do! I don't know because every
book is different, and because *I'm* different for every book.

I'm no longer the innocent young virgin I was (in the literary sense) when I wrote *One Sultry Summer* in Sicily and sold it
to Silhouette Books many years ago. My process has evolved,
and it keeps evolving. Moreover, my process for a 250,000-
word epic fantasy is different than it was for a 60,000-word
series-romance novel—as is my process for non-fiction, or my
process for a 100,000-word contemporary novel, or my process
for a 3,000-word short story.

In addition, the process that works for one big fantasy
novel doesn't necessarily work for the next. My pace is never
the same (*boy*, is my pace never the same!), my method of
construction has to vary, and even the way I coax my butt into
the chair for each project keeps changing.

So when people ask me all that stuff about how I
write...not only can I not fathom why anyone would want to
know this, since there is no right answer, no universal formula,
no secret handshake, and it's a pretty darn dull subject, anyhow...but I also simply *cannot answer*—no more than you can
answer (I hope) how you make love every time you do it. One
way or another, the books and the stories and the articles get
done year after year (just as, one way or another, the hormones
get exercised), and that's all that really matters.

So Harry Turtledove was right: It *is* like sex. I mean that
it's a private, special, individual process which often yields
a very public result (a book or a baby)—and which also
sometimes fizzles out into an awkwardness you don't ever
want anyone else in the whole world to know about (those
"what was I even *thinking*?" moments at the keyboard, those

"oh, let's have a drink and forget the whole thing" moments with your partner).

And, as a card-carrying I-don't-care-how-YOU-do-it novelist, I'm always amazed by how many accomplished writers (never mind aspirants) worry that their process isn't "right," that they're doing it wrong. If someone else writes in the mornings, or every day, or nine pages per day without fail, or three drafts of every novel, more power to them. I have written in the morning. I have written nine pages in one sitting; in fact, I once wrote thirty-five pages in one sitting, but I was younger and hardier then. However, I've never written three drafts of a book, and I think I'd rather eat ground glass than do so. And, yes, I've even been through phases where I wrote every single day.

And you know what? BIG FAT HAIRY DEAL.

What works for someone else has nothing to do with you or with me. I can't light up a cigarette when I get stuck on a tricky scene because, oops!, I don't smoke. (That's a *habit*, remember?) I do whatever the hell it is I have to do at that moment on that day with that particular scene. Sometimes I get cookies (because I *am* an adherent of the Elizabeth Bevarly Theory: There is no plot problem that cookies will not solve). Sometimes I circle the computer in chaotic despair for three days, sometimes I go back fifty pages in the manuscript to figure out where I went wrong, sometimes I scrap a scene (or a character, or a premise, or a plot thread, or even a whole story), sometimes I get hit with sudden inspiration (usually while I'm in six-lane traffic)—and sometimes I just sit there *wishing* I smoked.

One way or another, I just figure it out each and every time—though I'd be the first to admit that years of experience help, particularly in terms of confidence: "Come on, Resnick, you've done this a thousand times before, so I know you can do it now. Just hang in there." And that's not something I could say to myself as I composed my first-ever novel so many moons ago.

Only I can find my own way. Only you can find your own way. Only Stephen King can find his own way. We can grouse and share and commiserate all we want—in fact, it's fun to do so! But no one has the answers—and I recommend punching them hard if they say that they do.

No, you don't really have to punch them. Just be aware that *I* will. You've been warned in advance. Hey, I may not be a creature of habit, but that doesn't mean I'm incapable of planning ahead.

What I've Learned From Will

Like many unfortunate people, my first exposure to the works of William Shakespeare was in school. As a teenager, I was forced to read *Julius Caesar* in English class. Though a bookish kid, I was ill-equipped to struggle through Shakespearean language at age fifteen. ("Come hither, sirrah.") Moreover, as a modern American teenager obsessed with modern American teenage stuff, I was indifferent to the point of somnambulism when Marcus Antonius comes "to bury Caesar, not to praise him" in the brilliant eulogy which stirs up the masses and skillfully manipulates the crowd in this initial salvo of what soon becomes all-out war between him and Brutus, one of Caesar's assassins.

As Mark Antony laments Caesar's murder before the masses of Rome, he keeps insisting that Brutus and Cassius are "honorable" men who *surely* had good reasons for what appears to be their wholly unconscionable murder of Rome's greatest leader: "Er, *did* they have good reasons? Does anyone at this eulogy happen to know?" Unspoken in this scene is the fact that Antony's wagon was hitched to Caesar's star, making Cassius and Brutus his enemies, too—enemies who will oppose Antony's now picking up some of the power that dropped and scattered when Caesar fell.

Well, gee whiz, Antony tells the crowd, *he's* sure not going to accuse those two fine, upstanding men of vicious murder or base motives, no, indeed…And yet, as the scene progresses, Antony turns the crowd against them, bringing the people under his influence with the fluid skill of a brilliant conductor directing his orchestra: "Gosh, I really don't want to upset anyone by going into morbid detail about the assassination…But, okay, if you *insist*, folks, I'll draw you a diagram of who stabbed Caesar in what body parts and how he suffered. By the way, did I mention the Big Guy left you a little something in his will?" By the end of Antony's eulogy, citizens who favored Brutus at the start of the scene are now screaming for his head.

I learned from Will that characters don't always say exactly what they mean, and they may have goals quite different from what they're telling people they're after. The whole time Antony is assuring the crowd he just wants to lay Caesar to rest and walk away without blaming anyone, he's deliberately doing exactly the opposite. When I came back to this scene again a few years after I started writing, I learned more. Just as a character may lie to the reader, so a character may lie to everyone else while letting the reader in on the joke. Will was particularly fond of writing the latter kind of scenario, and it was through watching his plays that I began to develop an understanding of when and how this technique is effective. Above all, I realized that Antony dumps huge quantities of dialogue on us in this scene because he's trying to *accomplish* something with it. Will showed me that dialogue can also be action.

Antony's friendship with Caesar served his own ambitions; now his manipulation of the crowd serves him by winning them over to his quest for power against Brutus' faction. Will taught me to ask the question I now pose first and foremost when developing a character's motivations and intentions: What does he want most, and how far will he go to get it? Brutus was willing to kill to keep power from Caesar, and Antony was willing to go to war for power.

However, despite their enmity, Antony respects Brutus. After defeating him, Antony says over his foe's corpse, without irony, "This was the noblest Roman of them all." I learned from Will that the most compelling adversaries may be those who respect—perhaps even like—each other.

Being forced to read *Julius Caesar* at age fifteen, however, I didn't get any of this. I also had no idea I'd grow up to be a writer; in fact, growing up in a writer's house ensured that writing was the very *last* thing I wanted to do with my life when I was a teen. (Like Will's character Romeo, I am fortune's fool. If my own life were played upon the stage, as Will writes in *Twelfth Night*, "I could condemn it as an improbable fiction.")

Being forced to read *Antony and Cleopatra* in my first year of college was an equally dismal experience. Shakespeare was spoiled for me for years thereafter by turgid academic interpretations that made his stories as clear as mud and forced his work into cherished ivory-tower theories. What I learned from this, as well as from some other good writers whom my education ruined for me, is: Do everything you can (if anything) to prevent academics from "teaching" your work. And write a prohibition into your will in case the vultures descend after you're dead.

Now you may be thinking, "Not my problem, Resnick. I'm a popular fiction writer. Academics will never even acknowledge my work—apart from the occasional dismissive reference to 'that populist trash'—let alone ruin it for generations of young people by interpreting my love scenes as metaphors about the relation-ship between the state and the monarchy."

Hah! Well, think again! That's exactly what Will said, after all, and look what happened to *him*.

Okay, maybe not *exactly* what Will said; but Will was a working actor and playwright whose job was to keep the crowds coming back to the theatre show after show. He was the Steven Spielberg of his day. Will didn't give himself airs about becoming (as he is now often called) the greatest writer in the history of the English language. Will was just the Elizabethan equivalent of a pop-fiction writer with a very demanding release schedule. Think of him as Nora Roberts with a beard. (And four hundred years from now, academics will probably theorize that Nora Roberts' stories were actually written by someone else, the way they say it about Will now.)

Will tried to keep people in their seats by writing strong, well-crafted stories about compelling characters, like any good writer. Yet centuries later, teenagers all across America are cursing his name as they're forced to wade through *Macbeth* while their teachers tell them (brace yourself) this is GOOD for them because it's WORTHY LITERATURE.

I'm telling you, start re-writing your will today.

Speaking of *Macbeth*, that one was forced on me at sixteen. As a sensible adult now, I'm uneasy about the obvious ramifica-tions of this. Suppose a teenage boy wants his father's sports car, and his girlfriend is urging him to get it or she won't put out. Next thing you know, their English teacher shows them how it's done by walking them through *Macbeth*: "We can kill the Big Guy, make it look like natural causes, and no one will ever know. Then the throne [Porsche] will be ours! In fact, it's really our *right*. We shouldn't even feel bad about this."

I missed these implications at sixteen, but now I can't understand why tax-paying parents don't put their collective foot down about this and insist on their teens being "taught," say, *Two Gentleman of Verona* instead. Oh, wait, no, headstrong young woman runs away from home; perhaps not. *Romeo and Juliet?* Teen lovers deceive parents and wind up committing suicide. Oops. *King Lear*: "Let's lock up Dad and take over all his property." *Othello*: "I suspect my wife may have cheated on me, so I guess I'll run mad and murder her."

It's a challenge, finding a Shakespeare play to which we can expose the youth of today without risking personal damages.

What I learned from Will is that basic human truths persist century after century, and a story which portrays them always speaks to us. Historians can write that people were considered "adults" by adolescence in other eras; but Romeo and Juliet, though of marriageable age at fourteen or so, are clearly *children* in their story which was written over four hundred years ago. We recognize their impulsive passions, their lovesick stupors, and their dimwitted optimism because, oops!, kids that age haven't really changed much since 1595. We're not peering through the telescope of time when we watch *Romeo and Juliet*; we're gazing at a crystal-clear mirror and seeing ourselves and our children gazing right back at us.

I first started to "get" Shakespeare when I was attending drama school in England. Our Shakespearean text teacher was named Judith, and she was so old that rumor claimed she was Will's daughter (also named Judith). When Judith got to talking, she'd start rattling off Shakespearean characters, conflicts, scenes, speeches, and one-liners, going so fast she didn't bother to say which plays she was quoting. I occasionally got confused and thought she was talking about her relatives. In any event, Judith's job was not to teach us what Shakespeare's text "meant," but rather how to speak it without keeling over in a dead faint (those passages are *long*), and to ensure the audience wouldn't collectively say, "HUH?"

Soon after we met, Judith realized she needed to give me the lecture she gave to every acting student who had attended university: "Forget what they taught you about Shakespeare, it's rubbish. These are wonderful characters who should not be locked in an ivory tower. Shakespeare wrote for the masses in the pit. If he were alive today, he'd be writing for television. What's *Titus Andronicus*, after all? Sex and violence, violence and sex."

Personally, I don't really envision Will writing *Baywatch*, but you get the point.

I went home and read *Titus Andronicus* that night. Judith was absolutely right! Sex and violence, violence and sex. That's Shakespeare for you.

I also learned that even a great writer can do some pretty lame work at the start of his career. I certainly did, and at least I'm in good company. *Titus Andronicus* was one of Will's earliest plays, and, let me tell you, it sucks canal water. *Baaaaaaad.*

Nonetheless, despite a few turkeys here and there, Will's overall body of work consists of many stories that continue to be riveting and full of human truth.

I feel sure I'm supposed to say something about *Hamlet* at this juncture, since so many people think Danish Boy was Will's greatest character. I'll go as far as saying *Hamlet* contains some of Will's best word-crafting. There's a reason you can't go more than thirty seconds in *Hamlet* without hearing a familiar saying (and we're talking about a four-hour play!); Will wrote brilliant, quotable, shrewd line after line after line in that story. I learned from Will that how well the language is crafted *always* matters;

I'm not buying any of this "that's not really important in genre fiction" crap. Will crafted that brilliant language to keep the masses coming back to the pit; that's what a good writer does, like a composer who makes sure we all leave the concert humming one of his tunes.

On the other hand, I always spend most of the play wishing Hamlet would just shit or get off the pot. Has anyone in the whole history of the world ever vacillated as long and loquaciously as he does? Good grief.

However, though it's not my favorite story, it does contain some valuable lessons for me as a writer. Most notably, the famous (partial) line, oft-repeated to actors: "The play's the thing." The work I do is not about me, it's about the story; writers who forget to serve the story and instead try to make the story serve them are destined to deliver self-indulgent drek. And as Hamlet gives directions to the players, we hear the beleaguered voice of the writer, clear as a bell across the span of four hundred years, begging for some respect for the work: Just say the words the way they're written, don't gesticulate too much, "suit the action to the word, the word to the action," and, for god's sake, don't ruin my work by overacting (read: over-editing).

Anyhow, if I had to pick a favorite from Will's work—and I'm not sure I can, so don't hold me to this—I think it might be *Macbeth*, despite my trauma over being forced to read it at sixteen. Admittedly, sitting through that play is a hard day's night; you've got to be in a grand, tragic mood.

Macbeth and his wife kill a king who trusted them, in order to gain the throne with which three witches tempted them. But before long, the Macbeths find themselves in that "undiscovered country"—not death, which Hamlet fretted over, but conscience and consequences. They're gradually tormented by the weight of their guilt until their world falls apart. Lady Macbeth loses her mind, and Macbeth's self-loathing leads to such stark bleakness that he decides life is a tedious, never-ending "tale told by an idiot, full of sound and fury, signifying nothing."

What I love about *Macbeth* is how much I learn from it every time I sit through it. The story captivates me because, when it begins, I *like* Macbeth. The evil deeds of a villain are par for the course; but the evil deeds of someone we care about are compelling. Someone tormented by guilt and doubt, someone who longs to undo something he has done…This someone is *us* (even if, okay, we haven't committed regicide lately). Each time I sit through the first few acts, I find myself hoping that *this* time, Macbeth won't kill Duncan—or that *this* time, he can find redemption for doing it. Now *that's* good writing.

Macbeth makes me ask, as a writer, not only how far a character is willing to go to get what he wants, but also: How far is *too* far? What could make you go there? How do you know when you're finally there? How do you get back? *Can* you get back? Is remorse enough for forgiveness? Is sacrifice enough for redemption?

Will's body of work, stretching across the centuries, teaches me that the writer's most important work has always been exploring the human heart in conflict with itself. And four hundred years from now, I believe that will still be true. (So, really. Re-write your will.) In any case, it's our duty and our privilege to continue Will's work. As storytellers, we are "the abstracts and brief chronicles of the time."

Best of all, "We are such stuff as dreams are made on." And I learned that from Will.

Selling Elsewhere
Is the Best Revenge

One of my favorite novels, W. Somerset Maugham's *The Razor's Edge*, was once rejected by an editor who remarked, "I think it is distasteful." The novel not only became one of Maugham's most successful books (and, in my opinion, far and away his best), it was also made into a fine movie with Tyrone Power. A couple of decades later, another editor wrote, "You're welcome to [John] Le Carré—he hasn't got any future," after reading *The Spy Who Came in from the Cold*. The book became the first of the author's international bestsellers, and (like a number of his works) was also adapted as a major motion picture. Tony Hillerman, who is now as culturally admired as he is commercially successful for his series of mysteries set on a Navajo reservation, received this rejection some thirty years ago: "If you insist on rewriting this, get rid of all that Indian stuff."

Indeed, if you read *Rotten Rejections*, published by Pushcart Press, you'll find a huge variety of reasons that editors have given over the decades for rejecting works that went on to become classics forced on me in school, huge commercial best-sellers, and award-winning standard-bearers. Writers who now live as literary icons in our minds, and whose careers represent extraordinary commercial pinnacles, have often received rejections that would send a weak-kneed aspiring writer to bed with a bromide for a week.

As a not-infrequently-rejected writer myself, I find that fact so comforting that I was genuinely astonished, years ago, to see a letter in the *Romance Writers Report* from someone who thought *Rotten Rejections* was in bad taste because it called into question the judgment of editors.

Hull-o-o-o! Anyone home? Exactly!

For goodness sake, if writers *didn't* call editors' judgment into question, then we'd give up completely on a book the moment even one editor said, "It's no good." And what a criminal waste that would be! As writers know (and as I assume editors know, too), editors often say that sort of thing about work which then sells elsewhere—even about work which goes on to achieve considerable success. Editorial judgment is subjective, and editors are only human.

The eleven agents who rejected me at the start of my career certainly weren't the last people ever to reject my work; nor was that episode the last time I was later glad I hadn't let someone's negative opinion hold me back. On several occasions, eventual sale of a much-rejected novel has earned me a higher-than-ever-before advance.

No, I haven't sold all of my rejected work. Some of it did indeed prove to be unsaleable. But I've sold a lot of it. So every time I get a rejection, I think of that. I also think of Le Carré, Hillerman, Maugham, and the rest of the gang. In fact, few things inspire more professional courage in me than hearing about triumph in the face of adversity, e.g. a sale after many rejections.

For example, an agent told Lorraine Heath that her writing "lacks a vivid touch" and refused to represent her. *Sweet Lullaby*, the book that inspired this evaluation, sold three months later, made the Waldenbooks romance bestseller list when it was published, and became a finalist for the prestigious Rita Award. Jodie Nida's first novel was rejected "by everyone on the face of the earth," so she put it aside and broke into the business with other manuscripts. Ten years later, however, she revised that much-rejected first novel and sold it to Berkley Books as *Render Safe* (written as Jackie Nida).

Being rejected by every editor in the free world is not that uncommon in the hidden past of many published novels. Two Denise Dietz novels, *Throw Darts at a Cheesecake* and *Beat Up a Cookie,* "had a dozen rejections" before Walker bought them in hardcover and Harlequin Worldwide bought the paperback reprint rights. Robyn Carr's *The House on Olive Street* (which is about a group of novelists) picked up thirteen rejections before being acquired by Mira, where she has since sold a number of books. Jennifer Crusie's *Tell Me Lies* "was turned down a lot" before it sold to St. Martin's Press and went on to become a bestseller. In a particularly tidy twist of circumstances, at least two writers I know wound up selling their oft-rejected manuscripts to imprints which had previously rejected those books.

Career novelists are familiar with a fact of life that non-writers find incredible: Writers' *own* publishers often reject their publishable work. As bestseller Susan Wiggs says, "A rejection is an invitation to submit elsewhere." Even if your publisher discourages that. After all, unless your publisher offers to put you on salary with benefits, what right could they possibly have to ask you—an independent free-lancer whom they'll drop like a venomous serpent if your sales figures decline—to simply give up on work which they won't buy? It's not personal, it's business. If your publisher won't publish a book, take it elsewhere and see what happens. It could be well worth the effort.

Jennifer Crusie gives an example of a book, *The Cinderella Deal*, which Bantam bought after her own then-publisher, Harlequin, rejected it; it went on to become a Rita Award finalist. When my publisher Tor Books rejected a new series I proposed, I sold it elsewhere—for substantially more money than Tor had previously indicated it might consider offering. Candace Schuler explains that someone who was (very briefly) an editor at Harlequin turned down one of her books flat, with no room for discussion or revisions. Candace had done ten books with Harlequin by then and felt confident the book could work, but the editor was adamant. A few weeks later, Candace sold the book to Silhouette, where she actually made more money for it than she would have with Harlequin. The book also rose higher on the Waldenbooks romance bestsellers list than any of her previous novels. "Incidentally," Candace adds, "[that editor] is no longer at Harlequin. But I am." When Sherry-Anne Jacobs' Australian publisher changed management, they sent back a book which the previous editorial director had told her they were going to buy; they also told her not to submit to them again. The book not only went on to sell in the U.K. and the U.S., but it has been reprinted several times (meanwhile, the Australian publisher is under new management yet again).

Far more disruptive to one's schedule and income, of course, are editors who reject contracted novels after they're completed and turned in. Numerous writers have told stories over the years about this happening after they were "orphaned" when the acquiring editor left the publisher; but sometimes the acquiring editor is the one who deems the delivered manuscript to be unpublishable. This is where the writer must find a whole new level of emotional endurance and self-confidence (not to mention thrifty financial habits) if she is to triumph.

A very successful genre author changed houses at one point, one of her reasons being that the new editor was enthusiastic about her doing a different kind of book which had an edgy, challenging theme. The proposal "was accepted swiftly and without question." The author delivered the book...and the editor declared it unpublishable. "Ultimately, I did five major rewrites for that house (and went without income for a solid year)," the author says, but her efforts wrought no change in the publisher's steadfast rejection. However, once the book was finally free of that contract, two other publishers immediately made offers. The book went for a six-figure advance, had the author's largest print-run up to then, and did very well in the marketplace.

Unpublishable? Go figure.

Fantasy novelist Jennifer Roberson shares a similar tale. Her agent submitted an outline and chapters for a "meaty, mainstream novel of history, romance, and politics" set in seventeenth century Scotland. Instead of the one-book deal the agent proposed, Bantam was impressed enough to offer a three-book six-figure deal.

However, after Roberson turned in the book, the editor told the agent that the first 300 pages, fully one third of the manuscript, were "crap" and had to be cut. "I was stunned," Roberson says. "I'd given them what the outline promised, and what my agent had discussed with them in view of building a mainstream historical career with Bantam." Aware that the author is not always the best judge of her own work, she asked her agent to read the book. He agreed with her that the first three hundred pages of the book were not "crap," and that to eliminate them completely would destroy the story. Bantam, however, remained firmly convinced that the book was unacceptable without the major cut they wanted, and so Roberson and her agent cancelled the contract. Very soon thereafter, Kensington made a two-book offer, with an on-signing advance that enabled Roberson to pay back the original advance to Bantam. Requested revisions were minimal, and the book, *Lady of the Glen*, has performed well in hardcover, trade paperback, and mass market paperback.

"What I learned from this experience," Roberson says, "is that money is no substitute for trusting one's heart and the luxury of living without even a trace of regret for What Might Have Been. Authors must be true to themselves—and to their vision."

Sometimes, however, being true to one's vision has very peculiar results. A writer I know used a pseudonym to write a novel set in the 1960s with a black male protagonist. One of the publishers to whom it was submitted offered a six-figure advance...but only if the author was available for tour. During this discussion, the author's agent realized that the publisher assumed that the author was a black male writer in his mid-fifties who had lived through the events described in the novel. After discussing this with the author, the agent called back and told the publisher the truth: "The author can tour, but she's a white woman in her thirties." The publisher told the agent they didn't want the book, after all, and withdrew their offer.

The author adds, "We did manage to sell the book under a pen name to a mystery house for a lower-than-hoped-for five-figure advance. No touring."

However, as peculiar as that tale may seem, here's an even stranger one. One writer got a rejection letter from a Ballantine editor which said, "Something about the manuscript made me sneeze. That might have been one of my problems [with it]." The novel went on to become the launch book for another house's romance program, was reprinted several times, sold in nine countries, and has earned out at six-figures for that author.

Finally, for someone out there in the middle of what seems like a very long slump of perpetual rejections with no hope in sight, please consider the experience of a novelist whose career bottomed out after a couple of books due to a variety of circumstances which included her editor being replaced by someone who didn't like her writing, her then-agent (later sued by many former clients) wasting a great deal of her time, and a major market slump in the author's genre. Then, after eight years without a sale, this writer clicked with an agent she met at a conference. The following year, he got her under contract with two major publishing houses, one of which had previously rejected one of the books he now sold them. The author has been continually under contract ever since.

So pick yourself up, dust your book off, and keep on trying. Who knows what could happen?

Gunk

Writing is like yoga.

It's also like sex, cooking, parenthood, opera, war, gardening, and conjugating French verbs. But we're going to go with the yoga analogy for now.

In my yoga class, my teacher tells me to think about my rib cage, my thigh muscles, my spine, my breath, my gaze, my ankles, my mouth, my cheeks, my hands, my balance, my toes, my belly, my kidneys, and The Universal. She also, at the same time, tells me to clear my mind and think of nothing. Then she tells me to stand on my left earlobe.

I'm sure the obvious parallels to writing are instantly apparent to you.

Everything and nothing is going on at once. In my yoga practice, I seek to achieve a simple purity, a place of no expectations or worries...which cohabits with the interlocked complexity of a world-embracing wholeness—while also striving to put my calves in the creases of my elbows and levitate. (No, I'm not even close to achieving that pose.)

Writing a novel is a combination of craft and art, precise objectivity and organic instinct, academic discipline and freewheeling deep play. It requires a master carpenter's flair in using a large toolbox of learned skills, including plot and structure, pace and transitions, prose and dialogue, character development and subtext, grammar and vocabulary, and so on. Writing a book demands research skills, thousands of decisions and judgment calls, patience and persistence, and a long, detail-oriented commitment from the author. On top of all that, you've got to have a *story*, as well as a passion for telling that story. Additionally, there must be a commercial or "universal" component to this work, a reason that tens (or hundreds) of thousands of total strangers will spend their money and their time to read your book.

Finally, before you can stand on your left earlobe or levitate as a novelist, so to speak, you have to be able to concentrate and focus. No one has ever managed to write a novel while thinking about something else.

This is where purity comes in. Simplicity. The void which your talent and imagination fill, just the way my yoga teacher is always telling me to fill my lungs while trying to touch my toes to the back of my head. (No, I have not even got a toe off the ground yet.)

Yoga teachers and yoga books say over and over that the most important part of yoga practice—and the one that many students tend to undervalue or even skip—is *savasana*, which means (rather unnervingly) "corpse pose." As it happens, this is my favorite pose, and I have no trouble holding it for up to fifteen minutes at the end of class. That's the pose where you just lie there on the floor and rest. Now *this* is my kind of yoga!

When I was brand new to yoga, I thought I was really *good*

at lying on the floor like the dead. I thought that this was one pose I had down pat from the very start. However, now that I have reached a point in my practice where I can do one or two of the easier upside-down poses without falling on my head *every* time, I have begun to realize the truth about *savasana*: It's a LOT harder than it looks.

For the first minute or two of *savasana*, I am totally immersed in my pose, just grateful to be lying there doing nothing. For that time, I am simple, pure, a void, a clean channel through which The Universal flows.

But then I recover my breath and remember where all my body parts are, and before you know it...I start thinking about my grocery list. Or the infuriating e-mail I got just before leaving home for yoga class. Or what I need to write that day. Or my dwindling bank account. Or the IRS. I wonder if I'll get a parking ticket, because the meter always runs out about twenty minutes before class is over. I think about the notes I should prepare for a new writing workshop I'm supposed to give in a few months. I think about my deadlines. I mentally rehearse the conversation I want to have with my editor that afternoon. I start writing dialogue in my head for an upcoming scene in my manuscript.

I do everything but *savasana*. Everything but soak up my own energy in a place of mental peace and stillness.

It is in practicing *savasana* that I discover over and over how loud and persistent are the voices in my head. Even the really mundane ones, like, "Get milk. Buy bread. Phone your mother."

These voices are an example of gunk. (No offense intended to my mother.) The challenge of *savasana*, the discipline practiced in this pose, is to eliminate gunk.

Gunk gets in the way. It's a roadblock on the path to

enlightenment. In fact, gunk stops all *sorts* of things from functioning. Gunk once did so much damage to my spark plugs that it cost me nearly $700 to fix the problem. (My mechanic advised me not to let them get so gunky again.) Gunk makes my garbage disposal malfunction. Gunk got into the plumbing system of my previous apartment building, and two plumbers spent about thirty-six hours tearing my walls apart, removing my toilet, filling my bathtub with sewage, and running noisy mechanical equipment through the building's pipe system from the vantage point of my dressing room.

I'm going to go out on a limb and say that gunk is bad.

Gunk is also the voice in your head that says: "This book sucks." Or: "I have no talent." When you chew yourself out for not having written a full "X" number of pages that day; when you're distracted from the work in progress by worries about what reviewers will say about it as a finished, published novel; when the fear of rejection paralyzes you to the extent that you can't write; when you can't focus on your work because you're so demoralized by another writer's seemingly overnight success or by a disappointing response to your previous book...That's gunk.

Gunk is the roadblock we erect between ourselves and our goals. It stands between me and the focus I need to work on a book.

It's hard to write around gunk. Gunk clogs the channel, it muddies the stream, it fills the void with that sticky substance that traditionally belongs on the floor of a taxicab. When gunk invades your thoughts, it invades your writing space; and, thus, a place that could be infinite in its light and liberation suddenly becomes a small, dark closet that you're stuck sharing with a barnyard animal that hasn't been washed in quite some time.

My yoga teacher often reminds me that I am perfect just

as I am and that perfection is not static but ever-changing. I'll be different next year than I am now, but I'll be perfect then, just as I am perfect now. If I can't even get my toes off the floor today, let alone bring them to the crown of my head while melting my heart toward the ground, that's fine; toes-on-floor girl is who I am today. It may not be who I am tomorrow (although, realistically speaking, it's probably *exactly* who I'll be tomorrow), but it's who I am today; and today I am exactly who I'm meant to be. Tomorrow I'll be exactly who I'm meant to be, too. And I will only be toes-on-head girl when I'm ready, when that's who my perfect self is meant to me.

My point, and I do have one, is that the mental disciplines taught in yoga are about eliminating gunk. When everyone else in class is holding a beautiful balancing pose that I, toes-on-floor girl, can only achieve by employing the modification of leaning my butt against the wall, this is who my frigging perfect self is today. To compare myself negatively with others, or to fret about when (if ever) I'll be able to do the pose without resorting to this frankly unattractive use of the wall to help me...well, that's gunk.

Gunk says to me, "You look stupid right now. Aren't you humiliated?" And: "You could have this pose by now if you weren't too lazy to come to class more often!" And: "You're too fat for this pose." Note that gunk often contradicts itself from sentence to sentence: Could I get this pose if I came to class more often, or am I too fat to get this pose at all? There is no answer, because gunk is not a logical premise, it's *gunk*. Its sole function is to clog the channel, to block the path, to get in my way.

Gunk comes from me and no one else. Everyone else in class is too busy trying not to fall on their noses to pay any attention to what *I'm* doing (and anyone unfocused enough to be watching me is certainly not mastering her own pose anytime soon), and my teacher is enthusing with apparent sincerity about how beautiful my pose is. So my self-made gunk is the only thing standing between me and perfection just-as-I-am, butt against the wall and all. And one thing I've learned by now is that I won't ever achieve my pose while gunk is in my way. Progress in my yoga practice is only possible *without* gunk. (I fell on my head quite a few times before learning this.)

Similarly, I can't write a good chapter, a strong scene, a powerful climactic event while gunk is saying to me, "This material sucks. This book's not as good as the last one. You should be writing faster today. You should have written more yesterday. You're screwing up." And so on. Even gentler gunk is still counter-productive: "What will readers think of this book? What will reviewers say? Will I win an award for this book—or even be nominated?"

When I'm thinking about all that gunk—about how lazy and disappointing a writer I am, or about whether I'll be lauded and admired for my breathtaking work of staggering genius—what I'm *not* doing is getting my toes off the floor, let alone bringing them to the crown of my head. I'm nowhere near standing on my left earlobe, never mind levitating. Because I am not thinking about the *story*. I am not focused. I'm not centered fully on the work at hand. My channel is clogged. My creative space is full of the foul stuff that those plumbers pulled out of the wall of my apartment building after thirty-six traumatic hours last year. Gunk is in my way.

Happily, though, since gunk originates here—no middleman, no waiting!—I can *eliminate* it here, too.

Some of the most common ways that writers have told me they eliminate gunk are remarkably similar to what we're taught in yoga class. When asked about clearing gunk off the road of creative productivity, Robin Graff-Reed, author of seven historical romances (most of them written as Robin Wiete), who recently completed her PhD in clinical psychology (and therefore these days gets a *lot* of questions along the lines of, "How can I make the bad man go away?"), recommends that we cultivate positive affirmations, eliminate negative self-talk, and steadfastly avoid comparing ourselves unfavorably to others.

"Positive affirmations" doesn't mean saying something like, "I am a wealthy, world-famous, wasp-waisted bestseller" if you're not; that's not positive, that's just plain silly. It means reflecting affirmatively on what's truly positive about you. For example, "I am a good writer." Or: "I am an accomplished professional; I've completed previous writing projects and can complete this one; I am happiest when I'm writing steadily."

Eliminating negative self-talk means *not* saying things like, "I'm not as dedicated to my writing as I should be," or, "I've only published two short stories, and neither of them was that great." An example of unfavorably comparing yourself to others would be: "Betty Bigshot started writing at the same time I did, but she's sold a book, and I haven't. I should be where she is." Hey, if you're concentrating on Betty's pose, then you're not focusing on your own pose; and that's going to get in the way of your achieving it.

Prolific romance novelist Katherine Garbera says, "I have a list of affirmations that I keep posted next to my computer, and reading through them always helps to put me back on track. I also go back to the books I've written that I really liked everything about, the characters, the story, the writing process…That puts me in the right mind-set to write." She adds, "I also take time to remember the things I know are my strengths and focus on those."

Focusing on your strengths is like focusing on your breath; it's a centering technique. It starts pulling everything into alignment and creating a calm space where your pose can flourish, where your creativity can run free. My strengths as a publishing professional include persistence, endurance, and versatility. My strengths as a writer include structure, character-ization, dialogue, action, and humor. The more I remind myself that I have these strengths, the stronger they are able to get.

I seldom experienced gunk as a young writer. Despite a lot of career problems, I was consistently pretty prolific and productive. So I was unprepared when gunk blocked my path later on in my career. I didn't even recognize it until I was already neck deep in it. The floor of my creative taxicab became so sticky that I couldn't move. I was like a mouse stuck in one of those horrible slow-death traps. I went more than a year without being able to make progress on a book that was under contract and, needless to say, increasingly late. Several factors contributed to this situation, but gunk was certainly one of them.

Katherine Garbera says one of the ways she keeps the creative path clear in a difficult situation is to look at herself and her writing and ask, "What can I control?" At my nadir, I finally did this, too—and decided that gunk was one of the things of which I could take charge. I could start focusing on my pose and my breathing. I could work on silencing the dis-tracting, destructive chatter in my head. I started using positive affirmations for the first time in my life.

I did this in tandem with another creative survival tech-nique advocated by my friend Lynn Miller, who's published a number of books as Meg Lacey in addition to spending many years as a producer and media writer. As Lynn says, you can make choices to set yourself up for accomplishment rather than for failure. She points out that sometimes big goals get in the way of small goals, of the step-by-step things we can accomplish on the path that's heading in the direction of our larger goals.

During my period of gunk-filled paralysis, I repeatedly set myself up for failure. For example, I kept setting daily page-count goals of five, seven, ten, or fifteen pages at a time when I hadn't been able to write even ONE page for quite a while. This was plainly self-destructive, and yet I kept doing it. Then I would castigate myself for failing, for being a loser, for screwing up, for endangering my career. I'd accuse myself of laziness and self-indulgence. I did this over and over. I kept doing it even though it should perhaps have become apparent to my perfect self after months of not accomplishing anything that these habits were not working out well for me. (But, as already noted, I have to fall on my head a lot to learn these things.)

So, after far too much of this, I finally decided to set myself a goal that I knew I could achieve. Indeed, a well-trained poodle could have achieved it: I set a goal of working on the book for three hours per day, five days per week. Of course, I *could* have set a goal of working on the book nine hours per day, seven days per week...but I had fallen on my head enough by now to realize that that would just be setting myself up for more failure and would therefore be unproductive.

By "working on the book," I mean that I had to focus on it for three hours. If that just meant reading and re-reading the sixty pages that I'd written before entering my creative death spiral, or reviewing my notes and my outline, or staring at the screen and trying to think of one new sentence, that was perfectly acceptable. As long as I did this for three hours, I was meeting the goal I had set, I was *successful*. And during that time, I couldn't check email, answer the phone, go to the mailbox, or make a grocery list. Those three hours were sacrosanct, devoted totally to focusing on my pose and my breathing.

Moreover, my deal with myself was that every single time I achieved this goal, I *had to* congratulate myself. I had to say positive, affirming things: "You focused on the book for three hours today, Laura! Well done! Way to go! Good job! You're achieving your goals! You're swell!" (Mind you, I said all this *silently* to myself; but I said it.)

Well, after about three weeks of success, I got really daring and increased my daily-time goals to four hours per day. Then five hours. Finally, one day—after having sat with that book for so long in the positive, pressure-free, I-am-perfect, I-am-exactly-where-I'm-supposed-to-be-in-my-journey-today mode that I had created for myself as a last-ditch resort—I finally felt able to write a few sentences. After several days of this, I could even write a few paragraphs. My writing productivity gradually increased until one day I realized that I'd written nine pages that day. After another week or two, I no longer needed to set achievable time-goals, I was simply going into the office and writing away on a regular basis—the way I used to do, before gunk got in my way.

I was standing on my left earlobe and levitating!

I had gotten past the obstacle in my path. I had managed to eliminate the gunk. It's a lesson I've never forgotten—which is important, because gunk is always trying to creep back into my creative space. (Actually, even my yoga teacher gets distracted and falls on her nose every so often.)

There are many possible variations on how gunk strikes a writer. It may not occur as paralysis or burnout. Perhaps gunk turns one writer's process into something so painful it affects her personal life or her health. Perhaps another writer's gunk keeps her stranded in writing material that no longer satisfies her; or perhaps gunk prevents her from taking the risks she wants to take with her work. (It took me a while to push enough gunk out of my way to attempt my first upside-down yoga pose: "I'll fall; I'll look stupid; I can't do that; I don't like being upside-down; I'm scared; I don't know how.")

There are also many variations on how to move around, past, through, or over the gunk blocking a writer's path. I've cited here some of the techniques that have worked for me so far, such as positive affirmations, setting achievable goals, eschewing negative self-talk, focusing on your strengths, and avoiding comparisons with others. Since gunk is both insidious and sticky, I will continue seeking new ways to overcome it. And I will continue asking other writers confronting gunk to share some of their own discoveries with me.

Lions by Night

So I'm watching a forgettable romantic comedy on cable TV one night, and the male love-interest is an aspiring novelist who, like all his friends, is very impressed that he has (wait for it!) written a book. Completed a whole manuscript! Actually "done it" rather than just *talk* about it (which seems to be what all his friends settle for doing).

I reserve judgment and keep watching.

In a later scene, his novel has been "rejected by yet another publisher," and the heroine finds him slurping booze, flinging manuscript pages into a blazing fire, and feeling terribly sorry for himself as he decides to quit writing.

Well, a writer's world is inhabited by lions, and—oops!— this fellow is clearly a baby gnu (wildebeest). Most gnu calves get eaten on the African savannah right in front of their mothers. So I change the channel—but not before I say to the character, "Better run home, Gnu Boy, before the lions get you."

(Okay, yes, another secret's out: I talk to the TV.)

If you and I got that melodramatic every time we got rejected...Well, we couldn't be writers, that's for sure.

Who are you? Who made you what you are? What separates the long-distance runner from the mere dabbler?

As an aspiring young romance writer, I wrote three complete manuscripts on spec to warm up. Yes, I know, this is nothing. In my current local writing community, one of the romance genre's hottest rising stars wrote ten manuscripts to make her first sale, and another of my friends wrote more than that (and has since sold twenty books). They broke their backs to break in, instinctively knowing that total commitment was the least of the things they'd have to give. So did I.

And, if you're a pro, so did you.

I will boast a little about my fortitude, however, by adding that I wrote my first three manuscripts by hand, then typed them on a manual typewriter before sending them from Italy to the U.S. via trans-Atlantic surface mail...How long ago it all seems now.

Anyhow, I was hoping that, with three manuscripts in submission, I would at least see enough consistent comments in my rejection letters to help me improve upon my future efforts. As it happened, though, Silhouette Books bought my first manuscript—but not before eleven (count them, Gnu Boy: eleven) agents whom I queried all rejected me. However, at least the agents' comments had some of the consistency I had hoped for. Half of them said (I paraphrase here) that I had no talent and couldn't write. (Run if you're already bleeding, Gnu Boy, because their claws aren't even out yet.) The other half said that maybe I could write, but the romance market was dead, and I should try writing something with a bright future—like horror, for example.

(Soon thereafter, the horror genre entered a prolonged market nosedive, thus demonstrating that the words "agent" and "savvy" are not necessarily synonymous.)

As soon as I signed with Silhouette, my editor quit. Then my next editor quit. (Is it something *I* said?) Then I got an excellent editor...who promptly rejected four of my next six proposals and wrote me epic-length revision letters on the two she bought. Actually, it's thanks to her that I know about things like structure, conflict, and point-of-view, all of which were pretty foggy concepts before then.

(Where are you going, Gnu Boy? The fun is only beginning!)

Throughout my stretch of full-time self-supporting writing for Silhouette, they rejected at least half of my proposals. I eventually became unhappy writing series-romance, but almost everything else I wrote was rejected by every editor in the free world. I found solace in writing science fiction/fantasy short stories, which I first began doing soon after completing my eighth romance novel. The new challenge and variety of short fiction in another genre refreshed me enough to keep writing the books that paid my bills, but I felt I was in a maze and couldn't find my way out.

Meanwhile, of course, I was routinely treated to condescending comments from aspiring writers, none of whom had ever even completed (never mind sold) their Great American Novels. One fellow even suggested I should spend my advance monies learning "real" writing in a Master of Fine Arts program, so I could make something of my life.

Anyhow, one day I hit the wall. I decided I had shed enough blood on the savannah. I was tired, burned out, done. I abandoned my career and decided to spend nearly a year crossing all of Africa overland. (Well, it made sense to *me*.)

So there I was, shooing a warthog away from my tent in Kenya one evening, when a letter from Silhouette caught up with me, officially terminating our relationship. Enjoy irony? I received this news the same day I learned that *Romantic Times Magazine* had recently, at their annual awards ceremony, named my tenth book for Silhouette as the best of the year in its imprint (a field of more than seventy novels). However, my long-term sales had, by then, proved that my writing was unsuited to Silhouette's market. We parted on friendly terms (yes, really), and I've always stayed in touch with the fine editors I knew there.

Then while I was in Zimbabwe—trying, without success, to place an international phone call—my secondary publisher, the little-known Meteor, folded. While I was in South Africa, drunkenly evading some feisty elephants one memorable night, I won the John W. Campbell Award (Best New Science Fiction/Fantasy Writer) at the World Science Fiction Convention being held halfway around the world. I was less encouraged by this recognition than you might suppose, though; after all, *Romantic Times* had named me Best New Writer in series-romance once upon a time, and look how *that* had turned out.

(Newsflash, Gnu Boy: Writing well isn't the final goal, it's just the first step.)

I reached the Cape of Good Hope and, short of swimming to Antarctica, knew my odyssey was over, and the time had come to resolve who and what I was. I returned home quite broke, forever changed, and bearing an interesting assortment of scars. And I tried not to write. I tried really hard. (I also tried to get used to showering regularly and using toilets again.) Writing was a life that had taken only a few years to eat my heart, and I wanted to give it up. But I couldn't.

And neither, I'll bet, can you.

Who are you? Who made you what you are?

I never wanted to write. Born to a writer's household, I knew what awaited me if I followed that road, and so I took every detour I could find—yet I wound up selling my first book at twenty-five and never escaping this life thereafter, despite at least two genuine attempts to quit.

No, I can't quit. And maybe you can't, either.

When I first started writing professionally, my life was full of friends and family members all snickering about how I had always insisted I would never write, all saying to me: "I knew you'd write. I always knew you'd wind up writing." When I came home from Africa and, after several months of insisting I wouldn't do it, started writing again, new friends were now snickering alongside the old. One night, when I was still in my "I'm through with writing" mode, I wanted to hit one of my oldest, dearest friends who said to me: "I don't know all your future holds, but I know you'll always write, whether or not you accept that right now. That's who you are, and there's nothing you can do about it."

And if there's nothing you can do about it, either, then tough luck.

(What about you, Gnu Boy? Ready to feed your heart nightly to the lions, too?)

Fast-forward to my return to active writing status. Life soon becomes business as usual for me. A brief random sampling of typical events:

My next publisher lays off my editor and closes down the imprint; no one there ever answers my calls again. I write a new two-book proposal that's so unsaleable I suspect my agent of shedding tears over it. On another project, some editor says it's an insult that I submitted such a piece of shit. (Yes, really.) I write a three-book proposal so unmarketable that my floor nearly collapses under the weight of the rejection letters.

At some point, I make my second genuine attempt to quit writing. I get accepted into graduate school; but when I spend two days visiting the campus, everyone I speak with—students, advisors, professors, administrators—assures me the program is so intense that I won't have time, for the next two years, to write. Suddenly, my right arm, the endurance athlete of so much long-hand prose, can't seem to fill out the enrollment form. Maybe one day I'll be ready to go two years without writing; but not today. Today, I cave in and send my regrets.

Next, I sign to write some epic fantasy…and my brain turns to boiled jelly by the time I complete the 700,000-word story arc. My reward, as they scrape me off the walls like so much protoplasm, is to start another book; one which I have to write faster this time.

So, sure, I've seen some rough times. Yeah, I hear you: Big fat hairy deal. (Wake up and smell the river, Gnu Boy! You have to bring true grit to this party if you want to party here.)

I ponied up when true grit was called for, and if you've been working in this business for any length of time, so did you. However, I have a highly-developed sense of self-preservation, so, yes, I tried—I tried really hard—to leave the party when I discovered the "unconditional surrender" clause. I tried, but I'm like you: I cannot leave. I cannot quit. I cannot walk away.

Hey, you can try if you want to. Be my guest. After that initial burst of relief, that first flush of freedom, you'll be amazed at how hard it is. Believe me, I know.

Gnu Boy gets sloshed, weeps, flings manuscript pages

into a fireplace, and decides to quit writing because his very first book is rejected a few times. I meet a lot of aspiring writers who might not be as self-pitying as he is, but I still see their faces fall when they find out that completing one whole manuscript doesn't even meet the ante if they really want to play with lions. I hear indignation in their voices when there's no place left to send their sole completed book, when all it has evoked among editors and agents is a bland dismissal even more discouraging than vicious rejection. (After twenty novels, sixty short stories, and a handful of awards, I still get bland dismissals—not to mention vicious rejections. So go cry me a damn river.)

If I meet 200 aspiring writers in a given year, I know that 199 of them will probably never sell a book. If I meet two novelists who've recently sold their first books, I know that one of these writers is likely to disappear before long. So why am I, who genuinely wanted to escape, still here? Why are any of us?

Talent certainly matters, and luck may be a factor, but as night descends upon the savannah, they're irrelevant without total commitment, true grit, and…what was that other thing? Oh, yeah—unconditional surrender. To what? Why, to your congenital inability to stop writing—and to everything you'll endure to satisfy the song in your blood.

Who are you? Who made you what you are?

I can't eject the characters who invade my dreams by night and my thoughts by day. I can't stop the constant "what if?" that pounds through my veins as insistently as my own heartbeat. I can't escape the "and then" which pursues me down every dark path where I have fled from visions so strong they're sometimes like hallucinations. All so a *Kirkus* reviewer can dismiss me with a few contemptuous adjectives, an anonymous Amazon.com reader can complain I disappointed her, and my next door neighbor can snickeringly confuse "fantasy" with "erotica."

I can only surrender. And that's all you can do, too.

So I feed my heart to the lions by night, because I've learned that it just hurts more if I resist. I have no real choice about this, and neither do you. Where will you turn when there's no one left to tell your tales to? How long can the voices in your head deafen you before you have to write them down? How far can you run from the fantastic thoughts and bizarre speculations which will always, in the end, outrun you, catch you, and bring you to your knees, fumbling through the dust of the savannah for your pen?

No one can run that fast or far. Least of all me. I know because I've tried. I've tried hard.

When I was a young writer, I really believed it was a choice. I could give it up. I could walk away any time. I only did this because I didn't really know how to do anything else. But now I know the truth, and if you're smarter than I, maybe you knew it all along: I do this because I can't not do it. Even if I could do something else, I'd still do this. And so would you.

If you could stop because of rejection, you would. I have friends in this business who've endured two, four, eight years of continual rejection without a sale, but couldn't stop. If you could stop because your publisher's shredding your work to make it conform to production standards or adhere to marketing trends, you would. Hell, you're not a masochist, of course you would! If you really had a rational choice about this, you'd spray the lions with a high-power garden hose, pick your heart up off the savannah, and take it home to be coddled and cared for only by the people who love you.

However, that's not among your choices. You'd know if it was, because when you got "rejected by yet another publisher," like Gnu Boy, you'd sit slurping booze, feeling sorry for yourself, and quit writing. Just like that. Other people can do it. But not me. And not you.

So you give your heart to the lions, night after night, because somehow, when it feeds them, your hunger is satisfied, too. You'll tell your tales until dawn breaks, and you'll keep writing them down even after that, because you can't stop. You'll always want it, need it, hunger for it. You'll never quit, never give up. You may try to walk away. You may flirt with another life or sleep with another dream; but you'll always be married to this vice, this gift, this obsession, this insatiable passion to tell a story and, above all, to let the lions feast on it. To let them feast on you, on your heart, on your tale after tale after tale…Because if you could have kept it to yourself, you would have. You're not a fool.

Who are you? Who made you what you are?

Womb to tomb, you are a writer, a filthy pro, a storyteller. You are the endurance athlete of the imagination. And—cast the blame where you will, or listen to others taking credit—the truth is that *you* made yourself what you are. You accepted, from the first, that total commitment was the very least of the things you'd have to give. When true grit was called for, you met the ante and didn't fold when the stakes were raised…And when you found out about the unconditional surrender clause, you laid your heart upon the savannah and let the lions come.

-The End-

Acknowledgements

My life as an essayist began when novelist Terey Daly Ramin contacted me one day, while she was serving as editor of *Nink*, the journal of Novelists, Inc., and asked me if I'd like to write a monthly opinion column. For what I both enjoyed and endured from then on, I blame Terey.

Those who share the blessing and the blame include my subsequent *Nink* editors, as well as the editors I wrote for at the *SFWA Bulletin* and the *Romance Writers Report*. As lonely and meager a life as writing is, it would be even lonelier and pay even less (well, pay *nothing*, actually) if no one acquired the work—or occasionally said to the writer, in response to a newly-delivered piece, "Hey, this one isn't too bad!" (A writer lives on meager praise as well as meager funds.)

My friends, my family members, my acquaintances, and even total strangers—non-writers as well as writers—contributed to these columns over the years, whether they provided material and quotes when I requested them, or suggested column topics to me, or unwittingly sparked my sleeping lizard brain into active zeal during the course of daily life. I owe them all (but they'll have trouble collecting).

Among these people, I particularly want to thank the friends who often discussed column ideas with me, encouraged me in dark moments, or put up with my tail-chasing when I got mired and stuck in the middle of a topic: Mary Jo Putney, Toni Blake, Lynn Miller, Karen Luken, Valerie Taylor, Jerry Spradlin, Julie Pahutski, and Cindy Person. There are many others, and I hope you know who you are—but I have space limitations.

Above all, though, every single time someone called me, emailed me, wrote to me, or stopped me in the hallway at a writing conference to tell me that something in one of my columns really spoke to them, I felt a renewed energy to keep on working. Writing professionally is not like keeping a journal or a diary. Sure, I write for satisfaction and self-expression; but above all, I write to be *read*, to touch others, to be heard, to find something universal among us and to share it as best I can. Being reminded that my fellow writers were reading my columns and getting something out of them was always what fueled me to write the next one.

—Laura Resnick, 2007